D0720653

Loving Again

Loving Again

Advice on Dating and Remarriage for the Widowed

JOSEPH A. RYAN

ZondervanPublishingHouse
Grand Rapids, Michigan

A Division of HarperCollins*Publishers*

Loving Again
Copyright © 1991 by Joseph A. Ryan

Requests for information should be addressed to:
Zondervan Publishing House
1415 Lake Drive S.E.
Grand Rapids, Michigan 49506

Library of Congress Cataloging-in-Publication Data

Ryan, Joseph A., 1920–
    Loving again : advice on dating and remarriage for the widowed /
Joseph A. Ryan.
        p. cm.
    Includes bibliographical references.
    ISBN 0-310-53631-6 (pbk.)
    Widows—Religious life. 2. Widowers—Religious life.
3. Remarriage—Religious aspects—Christianity. 4. Dating (Social
customs)—Religious aspects—Christianity. I. Title.
BV4528.R92 1991
248.8'4—dc20   91–4339
                                                                          CIP

All Scripture quotations, unless otherwise noted, are taken from the HOLY BIBLE:
NEW INTERNATIONAL VERSION (North American Edition). Copyright © 1973, 1978,
1984, by the International Bible Society. Used by permission of Zondervan Bible
Publishers.

All rights reserved. No part of this publication may be reproduced, stored in a
retrieval system, or transmitted in any form or by any means—electronic,
mechanical, photocopy, recording, or any other—except for brief quotations in
printed reviews, without the prior permission of the publisher.

Edited by Bruce and Becky Durost Fish
Cover design by Art Jacobs

Printed in the United States of America

91 92 93 94 95 96 / AM / 10 9 8 7 6 5 4 3 2 1

Dedicated to
Joseph C. Ryan,
a widowed educator who dared to
remarry at age fifty-five and begin a
second family. He became my father when
he was sixty-five.

And to
Elsie Orcutt Ryan,
a previously unmarried educator
who had the courage to marry a
widower twenty years older than she and
bear him four children. I was the last of those
children, born when she was forty-five. Her death two
years later left me without mother memories, but her writing
life still lives through mine.

Contents

Foreword

For all too long an adequate, in-depth treatment of the concerns of the widowed has been missing. Scores of articles have touched on the pain of separation, starting a new life, and other related concerns, but few authors have tackled a cohesive book-length treatment of these issues. Thus it is with a great deal of satisfaction that I have had the privilege of reviewing *Loving Again* by my long-time friend and honored colleague, Joseph Ryan.

Joe, as we affectionately know him, and I worked together as administrators for the National Association of Evangelicals. He walked with me in the early days following my own wife's death, and he had some connection with the romance that led to my marriage with Lona Brubaker. Beyond that, he has interviewed many widows and widowers and empathized with the broad range of their experiences, some of which I did not have personally. Quite likely that is why this work has a note of authority that it would not have if it had been written by one who had experienced only one dimension of the sorrows and hopes of the bereaved.

Even as I write this Foreword, a close relative is going through the Valley of the Shadow of Death emotionally at the unexpected death of his wife of almost fifty years. He is reaching out for an understanding of the processes of life and is searching for answers. I was grateful to have in hand the early manuscript of *Loving Again* so that I could share with him the broad range of insights in the book.

Joe raises important questions and issues such as, Is there a place for romance in the days ahead now that a loved one is gone? What does dating mean at this stage of life? How does one go about courting when one is older? What commitments and sexual issues need to be faced? How will the families on either side react? Joe's answers are not only definitive, but wise.

I hope that all readers will profit as much as I have by reflecting on these issues and answers. As a former seminary dean, I can say that *Loving Again* will be useful as a collateral work, or even as a textbook, for seminary professors who prepare students for pastoral and other Christian ministries. This work undoubtedly will be a classic in this area of Christian literature. Whether or not the reader has gone through similar valleys, he or she will profit by the reading.

Arthur M. Climenhaga, S.T.D., LL.D.
Former Seminary Dean and Church Administrator

Acknowledgments

Much of this book is drawn directly from the lives of remarried widowed persons whom I personally interviewed. Without them, the book would not be in your hands. Sometimes I relived painful memories with them. Other times our laughter filled the room.

While all names have been changed to protect their identity, the people in this book are real. Some were shy initially; others were eager to talk about themselves individually or as part of a couple. I am especially grateful for their sensitivity, frankness, and willingness to divulge details that were private and sometimes intimate. At the end of the interviews I often felt their reflective thought and conversation had served as a catharsis for them and helped redefine their past and future.

Other remarrieds who responded by mail to my questionnaire, along with psychologists, pastors, lay workers, librarians, and others, were valuable resource people.

Indispensable are those who can kindly but relentlessly critique a writer's efforts while his work is in process. Special thanks go to everyone in my critique group, led by Marion

Duckworth. My friend Mettie Williams was a helpful manuscript reader.

The first and last to see the manuscript was my wife,
Velma, who recognizes with me that we have yet to face the
experiences and decisions faced by the people in this book.

May the information in these pages help many thou-
sands of widowed persons avoid mistakes, find answers,
and—if it's in the plan of God—discover a new partner and
years of joy.

Joseph A. *Ryan*

Introduction

Guilt and anguish twisted Olga's face as she sat across from me in my church study. A cry for help was written across her distorted features. I was a young pastor and eager to help.

Two months before I had performed the marriage ceremony for Olga and George at the close of a morning worship service. They had been widowed in their early fifties. I had been preaching a series of messages from the gospel of John and had arrived at the wedding Jesus attended at Cana. The passage for that day spoke of a happy time, of God's concern for marriage, and of the support and encouragement friends provide.

Except for the couple's close friends, the congregation did not expect an on-the-spot wedding to illustrate the sermon that morning. Just before the benediction, I invited the wedding party forward and was pleased to see surprise and joy playing tag across the faces in the pews.

It was a simple ceremony with traditional vows, no music, and very brief remarks. After the wedding kiss, I gave the benediction and watched as delighted friends surrounded the couple. The California sun seemed to shine with unusual brilliance for them as they walked to their car.

Just how soon pain and disillusionment erased Olga's joy is not clear. My first hint was that afternoon two months later when I answered a knock at my study door, and she was standing there, alone.

I motioned Olga to a comfortable chair and sat across from her. After her first few quiet words, she could only look down at her hands. She twisted her handkerchief and tried to wipe her tears.

Finally I asked, "Can you tell me what's hurting you so much?"

"He wanted me to . . . to . . ." After groping for words, Olga found non-anatomical language to describe what was happening in her intimate love life. George was insisting on a type of sexual activity that horrified her.

"I can't do that!" Olga exclaimed. "What does he think I am?"

As we sat talking, less than twenty-five feet from where George and Olga had taken their vows, my happy memory of that wedding did a fast-fade to black. Despite my best efforts, Olga could not face life with such a man.

Little in my training had prepared me to provide help for Olga and George's conflict. I knew that the intimate details of marriage should have been discussed by them in advance, but I had not been taught how to lead such a discussion. There was nothing I could give them to read on the subject, and no qualified counselors were available to guide them toward reconciliation.

In the end, George left Olga and the marriage was

dissolved. Olga soon relocated and I was no longer her pastor.

I'm still haunted by the memory of George and Olga, and I wonder how many other widowed persons have faced the misery of damaged or failed relationships without any hope of adequate support and counsel.

Even today the help available for the nearly fourteen million widowed persons in the U.S. comes as a by-product of the massive attention given to divorce. Books, articles, television shows, movies, counselors, and support groups all provide support for those experiencing divorce or seeking remarriage.

While the widowed can find some help from these resources, they have many needs that are not addressed. Books for the widowed deal mainly with the grief process, financial considerations, and adjusting to the single life. No one seems to expect the widowed of any age to remarry. But they do, and they will.

During thirty-five years in Christian service, I have observed and supported many remarriages among the widowed, but I have not found much written to help them. This book was written to address that need.

Loving Again is intended for men and women who are experiencing the stirrings of love after being widowed. It is also for those who are already remarried and need reassurance or insight. Family members, counselors, and pastors who have contact with the widowed who have remarried will also find help and encouragement here.

Though I value the advice of professionals, the principal approach of this book is to let the reader hear directly from those who have ached, cried, survived the loss of a spouse, and begun a new marriage. These remarried couples talk openly about their struggles. Their experiences provide fresh insights into the lives of many others who are friends and family members. All of their names and any identifiable circumstances have been changed to protect their privacy.

Those interviewed represented a wide range of ages: the youngest, thirty-three; the oldest, nearly eighty. In keeping with the membership guidelines for the American Association of Retired Persons, I refer to anyone over age fifty as a senior.

Statistical realities play a crucial role in understanding the needs of the widowed. The following facts are particularly important to keep in mind:

1. Ninety-five percent of all widowed persons in the United States are age forty-five or older.[1]
2. Of those widowers who remarry, 86.5 percent are age forty-five or older. For widows, the number is 70.1 percent.[2]
3. In 1989, the average age of remarriage for widows was 53.0 years and for widowers was 60.8 years.[3]

Statistically, then, the widowed are an older population. Yet there are also those who lose a spouse by death in their younger years. They find the experience just as painful and the future equally difficult. Their unique concerns will also be addressed here.

Though this is not a theological work, it assumes a Christian world view. I believe in a God who loves us, cares about what happens to us, and has made provision for all our needs in the person of Jesus Christ. So do most of those interviewed.

Though they believe in God, the people you will meet in these pages are not perfect. Many of them wrestled through dark nights of grief and loneliness. Some faltered and made mistakes. However, when they emerged into the sunlight of a new day, they found that God had never left them.

The pastors, counselors, Christian friends, and adult children of the widowed need to hear what I heard in these interviews. Their stories and comments speak to the fundamental issues of life, love, and faith. There is wisdom in their words that can help all of us face the future with hope.

1
Coming Alive Again

In one episode of NBC's *Empty Nest*, widowed pediatrician Harry Westin drops by the lab in the medical center where his urologist-friend Eva is at work. She innocently asks if they have a date for that Friday night.

Harry: "A date? What do you mean?"

Eva: "Haven't we been having dinner every Friday night all these months?"

Harry: "We've just been having dinner together. I can't have dates; my wife just died."

Eva: "Harry, Libby died eighteen months ago."

Slowly, with a downward inflection, Harry answers, "Oh, but it seems like only eighteen days."

In fiction or in real life, the grieving process numbs and mystifies everyone. Angie struggled in the quicksand of grief for two years:

As a pastor's wife, I had trained myself not to let people know how I felt. If I was down, how could I counsel someone else? I wore a lot of masks. I could not be myself.

After my husband died, my mask was still in place. When I went to church I'd come home and cry all night. The trigger could be seeing some woman fifteen years older than I, coming into church with her husband. I'd say, "God, that's not fair! I'm only sixty-five and my husband's passed away."

Every time I went out I'd see things that hurt. Maybe some young couple. A guy would put his arm around his wife. I couldn't stand that. Here I was in church grieving, and my friends couldn't see it. Conscience made me go to church on Sunday morning; otherwise I didn't go out.

At home in the evening, I'd hear my husband's car in the driveway. Then I would realize it wasn't his car; it was the neighbor's.

At other times Angie would be the cheerful chauffeur taking a carful of women to a retreat:

On the way back, I could hardly stand it until I got home. When I was delivering these women, their husbands met them at the door and helped them with their luggage. All those things you never think about in advance happen. You see, I knew when I drove in my driveway, I would pull out my own luggage. When I was married I did that lots of times, but now there was no chance of someone doing it for me.

All these strange things were happening to me. I became a person I didn't know. Before, there was nothing Angie couldn't handle, some way. That was how I appeared to other people. I gave them confidence. Then, when it was my turn, I found I didn't have it myself.

The widowed person's agony is also visible in Sheldon Vanauken's A *Severe Mercy* when he spoke of his young wife. "How could things go *on* when the world had come to an end? How could things—how could *I* go on in this void? How could one person, not very big, leave an emptiness that was galaxy-wide? Everything—every object—was pervaded by the void."[1]

Whether it's Vanauken, Angie, or a person you know, their grief and pain are terribly real. Each experience is different, and any widowed person will tell you, "Unless you've experienced it, you can't know what it's like."

Coming alive again does not mean that all the grief is past, but that the worst of it is beginning to heal. The mental confusion and sense of unreality are receding, and some tentative social steps are beginning.

EMERGING FROM THE LOSS

Most counselors say that the experience of grieving the loss of a spouse will follow a basic pattern and produce certain specific feelings. At the same time, the process will be unique for each individual. The time taken for each part of the process will vary; some sections may occur in a different order and others may not occur at all. The following list of steps in the grief process has been adapted from several sources, but it most closely duplicates the pattern presented in Granger Westberg's excellent book *Good Grief:*[2]

1. Shock: A feeling of numbness and little comprehension of what has happened; a lack of emotions and an inability to cry.

2. Emotional release: The ability to let loose and weep freely, along with a desire to talk about the experience. Many people begin to seek help at this point. If an emotional release does not occur, there may be great psychological and physical damage.

3. Preoccupation with the deceased: An inability to release the mate that makes a person feel they are still married.

4. Symptoms of emotional and physical distress: Sleeplessness, an empty feeling in the stomach, and digestive problems. There may be shortness of breath and feelings of panic or a sense of unreality and a feeling that no one cares.

5. Hostility: It may be directed toward God, the physician, members of the family, or even the deceased spouse. Unresolved, it can turn into depression.

6. Guilt: The surviving spouse wonders, *Could I have done something that would have changed this situation?* He or she may feel guilty about some unresolved issue from the marriage.

7. Depression: There is much less activity. Despair, hopelessness, and unbearable loneliness begin to overwhelm the widowed person. This is often more intense for those who live alone and have no close family.

8. Withdrawal from friends: No social contacts. This common behavior can become destructive if it leads to substance abuse, promiscuity, overeating, financial irresponsibility, or a premature remarriage.

9. New relationships: Light shines through the gloom and life comes into focus again.

10. Resolution: There is a willingness to go on with life and to recognize that the process of healing will continue. The ache is still there, but waves of grief are less frequent.

The first six months after a person is widowed are generally a time of intense grief. This is followed by about eighteen months of residual grief.

The grieving process is affected when the widowed person has small children at home. "I felt the need to grieve quickly," Karen said. "Because of the kids I felt I had to get on with life."

Another widowed mother told me: "I always had to appear strong. If I would cry, that would upset the children. I often longed to have just one day for myself."

Eventually the winter of anguish ends. As daffodils tentatively push through the cold, crusty soil of spring, so frostbitten lives emerge from the process of grieving. But warmth is needed to renew the growth of the soul.

WARM CHURCHES

David, a businessman in his late fifties, was emphatic about where he found the warmth he needed to heal: "Right off the bat, church leaders told me I should go through the grief recovery class. The funeral was on Wednesday, and the following Wednesday was the first session of the class. I was there and finished the six-week course.

"Then a pastor's wife said, 'One of these days you'll have to get brave enough to come out to the singles group.' I figured I was just as brave as anyone else, so on the next

Tuesday I was there. The pastor's wife welcomed me and wanted to take me up to the front row where she was sitting. But I backed off; I wasn't that brave yet."

Both professional and volunteer care givers in churches provide valuable assistance for Christians who are working through grief. Trained lay counselors, very often other widowed persons, are increasingly used in this role. They are especially helpful when the grieving person has no family to turn to.

Another resource the church can provide is a network of previously established friendships. Neil, commenting on the loss of his first wife, said, "I think at that time you draw more from your Christian friends and your church. Even at the time of my first wife's death and funeral I felt a real closeness to our friends at church. That did more to help me than anything else."

WARM FAMILIES

Family members also play a crucial role in helping the widowed. "I had such great help from my family," said Nancy, who was widowed in her seventies. "My minister-son would come to visit often. He was the one I cried with. The minute he walked through the door, we hugged and cried. It was such a great outlet for me. It's not everybody you can cry with.

"I also had my daughter nearby, who was loving, kind, and thoughtful. She was constantly with me. Once a week we went shopping, and she included me in everything. Her three little sons were frequently coming and going at my place. I had my other children, too, and my brother and sisters. I was fortunate because I came from such a big family. Maybe that's the reason I didn't feel the need for counseling."

WARM LISTENERS

Though many churches today employ professional counselors, only four older persons I interviewed had sought psychological help for any extended period during their grief recovery. Each of them were in their forties or early fifties at the time of their loss. It appears that most people over the age of fifty view counseling with great skepticism.

Such skepticism was not evident in the widowed below age fifty. They seemed highly motivated to seek help from a professional listener. This was especially true if the loss of their spouse came through accident or suicide. When they had young children to care for, surviving parents felt an even greater urgency to get professional help.

WARMTH SHARED

Angie found healing by moving beyond herself and helping others. "After about two years of this [withdrawal and wearing a mask] I realized I had to get out and start doing things again," she explained. "Some of us [women] who were single started going out for dinner together, and that helped. We had somebody to lean on. Yet none of us would cry on each other's shoulders. We were all trying to wear our masks. It took several months of knowing each other before we finally had an understanding.

"If one called and said 'Let's go out for dinner tonight,' immediately all of us would say yes. We knew by the call that she was down, but would not admit it. At dinner we'd discover she was having a bad time. This was how we helped each other."

From this beginning, Angie and the others reached out to form a singles group in their church. This compassionate response to others showed that she and her friends were on the road back to personal wholeness.

Later, despite an initial reluctance to be associated with seniors, Angie began attending their dinners. Here she met Eric, a casual acquaintance whom she had not seen since college. As Angie put it, "a very gradual friendship developed."

Yolanda, the mother of two young children, was widowed in her thirties when her husband committed suicide. In spite of her responsibilities, she attended a grief recovery course and maintained a commitment to monthly follow-up meetings. To her surprise, she was invited to speak at a subsequent grief seminar. Next came a television appearance, and then other opportunities to share flooded in on her.

"The more I talked to other groups, the more it helped them and us [herself and her children]," she said. "After the initial shock and grief I did a lot of volunteer work; it made me feel better to help others."

WARMTH SHUNNED: UNHEALTHY WAYS
OF HANDLING GRIEF

Unfortunately, some people talk to no one. Perhaps the deep sharing of negative feelings with anyone is too threatening to them. Whatever the reason, they simply gut it out. Evelyn was like that: "I kept busy. I'm the quiet type and keep things to myself. I just kept everything in. I worked every day with no social life."

Being a silent stoic is painfully tough and can even lead to disastrous consequences. When the widowed become isolated in their grief, they can fall victim to all kinds of self-destructive behavior. Counselors generally agree that the following are the most dangerous:

1. Withdrawing from people, which eliminates account-ability.
2. Using any kind of drugs, including alcohol, to post-pone or dull the pain. The slogan of one grief recovery group is "Run now, pain later; pain now, heal sooner."
3. Using sex as a substitute for making peace with the pain, other people, and God.
4. Sleeping excessively or experiencing hyperactivity. Both are used to avoid dealing with feelings and making decisions.
5. Developing a clinging dependency that places the burden of grief recovery and personal decision-making on friends or family.
6. Overeating, which is an attempt to satisfy that inner emotional gnawing with food.
7. Entering into close romantic relationships too soon in an attempt to find comfort.

If a grieving person can avoid these traps, recovery will be quicker and scars will be less numerous.

EMERGING TOO SOON

The widowed risk real injury if they fail to complete their grief recovery before trying to go on with their lives. Those who have the support of close family or church relationships during the many months of recovery are least vulnerable.

An interrupted grieving process leaves many issues unresolved and this often leads to further emotional damage. There can be a tremendous hunger for love and affirmation. Loneliness may haunt the widowed. A crisis of confidence in God can lead to a total loss of moral values and a blindness to unhealthy relationships.

Though they were happily married when I spoke with them, a few people I interviewed had been vulnerable to the opposite sex during their lonely time of grief. Some had suffered through a disastrous second marriage before finding the healing touch of love with their present mate.

Norene, widowed in her forties, had a six-month marriage which ended in divorce. "After going through that experience," she said, "I know how needy a person is for companionship, warmth, and love. A warm body to be near. After you have lost someone and get beyond the first few months of numbness and it begins to wear off, there is this need. It's just a raw need, and I think that's why a lot of people run headlong into a new relationship."

Men seem to feel this need even more than women. They are often unwilling to go through a grief recovery class or even admit that they are suffering. Some try to keep up the macho image by refusing to cry.

They need to be reminded that godly men weep. Jesus cried over the death of his friend Lazarus (John 11:17–37).

When the patriarch Jacob died, his son Joseph "threw himself upon his father and wept over and kissed him" (Genesis 50:1). King David's tearful grieving over the loss of his infant son is one of the most poignant stories of the Bible (2 Samuel 12:13–22).

Many men have compelling reasons to weep. For them, an empty house can be especially devastating. Most women have friends they can talk to about their suffering and loss, but very few men have friends who can share their personal pain. The silence of the house smothers them. So they remarry quickly, without really knowing the other person or working through their own pain. Unresolved grief and incompatibility often send such remarriages to the divorce court.

WHERE IS GOD IN MY GRIEF?

Anger at God and a feeling that life is monstrously unfair are natural responses when we feel part of us has been torn away by death. But it will help us in our healing if we can recall God's past presence in times of confusion and rest in the assurance of his presence in our grief.

Jesus is described in the Old Testament Messianic verse of Isaiah 53:3 as "a man of sorrows, and familiar with suffering." In explaining part of his mission on earth, Jesus used some other words from the prophet Isaiah: "He [God] has sent me to bind up the brokenhearted . . . to comfort all who mourn" (Isaiah 61:1–2 quoted in Luke 4:18–19).

The British writer C. S. Lewis, who married late in life and then lost his wife to cancer, was well acquainted with grief. In retrospect, he thought it would have been better if he could have spent more time focusing on praise after his loss: "Praise is the mode of love which always has some element of joy in it. Praise in due order; of Him as the giver; of her as the gift. Don't we in praise somehow enjoy what we praise, however far we are from it?" Lewis was convinced that, "By praising I can still, in some degree, enjoy her, and already, in some degree, enjoy Him."[3]

Lewis found that praising God, even while grieving and questioning, restored his joy in God and his wife. Praise helped him realize that God had been with him all the time.

The same Bible that has given us insight and hope in good times, can be a spring of water for us as we wander in the desert of despair. From the familiar, "Even though I walk through the valley of the shadow of death . . . you are with me" (Psalm 23:4), to the less well known, "Never will I leave you; never will I forsake you" (Hebrews 13:5 quoting Deuteronomy 31:6), we are reminded that God hasn't left us in our tears.

As Lewis learned, it's during a time of loss that we rediscover who we really are: "God has not been trying an experiment on my faith or love, in order to find out their quality. He already knew it. It was I who didn't."[4]

In grief, we too will discover how much we love God and whether our relationship with Jesus Christ is intimate or casual. We may turn away from God, but he will never turn away from us, certainly not in the darkness of our grief.

At age twenty-nine, Elisabeth Elliot lost her first husband to the Auca Indians in Ecuador. She writes about loneliness, a companion to grief for the widowed: "The Lord has come to wipe away tears, the Bible tells us, and we may take that to mean He has come to dispel loneliness. He will dispel it—as soon as He can, not before. The tears, the loneliness, the pains of this life are a part of the process He is at work on. If we understand that, we need never be bitter about it. It will one day be exchanged for wholeness."[5]

It's hard to believe when grief is still fresh, but wholeness eventually appears on the horizon for the widowed. It even becomes possible to think the unthinkable: that renewed dating is possible. We'll develop some guidelines for dating in the next chapter.

HOW DO WE COME ALIVE AGAIN?

The process needs to include:

1. Sufficient time for grieving before any new steps are taken or decisions made. Moving too fast may short-circuit the grieving process and result in painful mistakes.
2. An awareness of the normal steps in the grief process and a commitment to avoid unhealthy response patterns to grief.
3. Positive help from the outside to address our specific needs.
4. A willingness to draw on all the spiritual resources at our disposal.

2

The Dating Game

As grieving recedes into the background and the widowed person begins to seek out new relationships, three basic issues need to be resolved.

First, the person must come to terms with singleness. David, who wasn't brave enough to face the singles group, said: "I didn't feel single at that time. Even though I had been through the [grief recovery] class and knew I was single, I didn't *feel* single yet."

Anyone who has been married for many years and then loses their spouse understands. It's the memories, the feeling that the spouse is still around somewhere. There is a sense of continuing dependence. The presence of children may speak of the former mate. Many confused feelings can mask the reality of loss or dull the sense of singleness.

Some say they don't want to feel single because that

would dishonor the deceased mate. This reaction clearly shows that the individual has not yet emerged from the grief process. Until the surviving spouse is comfortable with being alone again, it is too soon to begin dating.

Second, the widowed person must have an accurate picture of the previous marriage. Some widowed people deal with the pain of loss by glorifying or enshrining their deceased mate, others blame the deceased for all their suffering. Former mates are rarely either saints or scoundrels. It is better to focus on the truth about the relationship, with both its positive and negative sides. Real healing can only happen where the whole truth is known.

Larry described an experience he had when he started dating: "There was one woman who appealed to me. Her husband had been dead about four years, but she hadn't buried him. She was always talking about him. She even kept a big picture of him right on the TV while we watched." That woman was obviously not ready for another relationship.

For Christians who are serious about their faith, a sense of God's approval is a third element in any decision to date. Nancy, who had been single five years, told me: "I had a full life and wasn't looking for a second marriage at all. It came as a surprise to me, but I knew God was in it. I did not marry again because I couldn't stand to be alone . . . or was tired of being single. When I thought of remarriage I was excited because I could have fellowship with someone again. I realized I didn't have too many years left, and I felt life could be much fuller if I was blessed with a good companion."

Nancy had dealt thoroughly and maturely with loneliness. She had fully released her husband and accepted singleness as God's gift. This prepared her to accept remarriage as another gift from him. Her example suggests a healthy pattern for any widowed person. The amount of time to wait before dating is always determined by how long it takes to do the hard work of grief recovery.

PLAYING THE DATING GAME

There are many things a widowed person should know about dating, but the most important is this: It ought to be fun. Grim determination does not usually produce a healthy social life or happy remarriage!

No one should expect dating in their later adult years to be the same as it was in the teens and twenties. In most cases, it will be much saner and more enjoyable. At the same time, there will be some wild swings of emotions, both highs and lows. There will also be some dangerous traps waiting for the careless.

Dating should not always be seen as a process that leads to marriage. For some it will only serve to confirm that remarriage is not for them and for others it will be only a helpful social diversion. The Bible makes it clear that singleness is not second best, nor is remarriage the proper choice for all widowed people. The apostle Paul did not exclude anything when he said, "I have learned the secret of being content in any and every situation" (Philippians 4:12). That includes singleness.

Younger widowed persons face some difficult circumstances when they begin to date. Their own children may make it tough to carry on a normal social life. They may have no option but to date strangers, without any way of checking whether the person is trustworthy or not. Expressions of physical affection, like a kiss, may arouse unexpected feelings (though that can happen at any age). They may also worry about sexual expectations in general.

When there are young children still at home, a widowed person can feel imprisoned and harassed. Karen, widowed at age thirty-four with four small children, felt forced to do much of her dating at home. "The children tried to get between us [physically] and they hung on me all the time," she said. "Just having another man near me was hard for them. They weren't sure they liked him. If I had it to do over I'd go more slowly—perhaps go out more rather than seeing him at the house."

When Karen finally married Craig, she hadn't dated many other men. Among the young widowed I interviewed, this seemed to be the pattern. No doubt concern for the children's emotional well-being was a factor in their limited dating. Safe and competent baby-sitters are hard to find. Exhaustion from the dual role of parent and career-person also adds to the difficulty of maintaining the single-parent family and creates greater pressure to remarry quickly.

Determining whether a date has a stable and responsible personality is sometimes a problem. Yolanda, widowed at thirty-seven, described her first date this way: "I had a great time. It was a double date arranged by a friend. My date said he'd like to take me out again. But he never called. I was devastated. Later I discovered he was an alcoholic and suicidal. I kind of lost faith in my choices. I liked him a lot and it scared me that I could have fallen into a trap. So I've been really cautious."

Being "really cautious" is good advice for anyone who is dating these days, but it is particularly important for younger widowed persons. Most of them lack the stable social environment enjoyed by those who are older. They do not have a ready-made pool of relationships to draw on for "friendly" dates, and wise counsel is harder for them to find.

Older widowed people generally date someone from a familiar social group, whom they may have known casually for years. If they are about to make a bad choice, a friend in the group will often warn them. Irresponsible or predatory singles are usually discovered and removed from the group. This sort of dating within a larger social group, like a church, can also provide safety and support for younger widowed persons. Where past history is known and shared standards are respected, everyone is likely to be much better off.

Affection is an important part of dating and remarriage, but a first kiss often produces unexpected feelings. "I felt really sad after the first time we kissed," one young woman acknowledged. "It was like I was being unfaithful to my husband [deceased four years earlier]. I was depressed, but after thinking about it I realized that [my former marriage] was over and I had to move ahead. But it made me think of my husband, the good memories, and how I miss him."

The issue of sex can also create confusion and real fear in relationships. Lisa, a widow in her mid-thirties with two children, told me about some of her fears. "I went out a couple of times before dating Darryl [her present husband] and I didn't like it at all. I felt uncomfortable with my Christian principles and the sexual part of dating. Having been married and knowing all about sex, I didn't know what men would expect from me. So I just didn't date. I guess I assumed there would be expectations. For some reason, I didn't trust myself to set limits in a relationship. There was a lot of pain in my first marriage, with my husband's illness and the years we couldn't have a sexual relationship. It left me quite vulnerable."

Later, Lisa was finally able to set and maintain some standards for herself. "I wouldn't get sexually involved with anyone until I married. I dated only people I felt comfortable with. Then Darryl and I started dating on a friendship basis, knowing we were both lonely."

Establishing standards and maintaining them with the help of a supportive group of like-minded people is the real key to successful dating as a younger widowed person. It is also great advice for the widowed of any age.

SENIOR DATING

If the younger widowed face lack of accountability and isolation as their greatest difficulty, some older widowed persons, especially women, face statistical challenges that are equally daunting. After all, by age sixty-five, the ratio of women to men is about three to two and the widows in that older population outnumber widowers by five to one. As a woman ages, the statistical odds against her remarrying become even greater. Yet, many surprise themselves and do remarry. According to the U.S. Bureau of the Census, in March 1989 there were nearly 14 million widowed persons. About 100,000 of them remarry every year.

In American life, the pursuit of the perfect date has produced a wide range of support services. Computer dating services, personal want ads and even professional match-makers are all used to find the right person.

The people I spoke with were not interested in using such

aggressive methods and many of them wouldn't admit they were even looking for a date until they had found the right person. None of the older women interviewed admitted they were looking for a date or a mate in the beginning, and most of them were certain they would never remarry.

The older men were more active in looking for dates. They began sooner after their loss, and they usually thought in terms of courting from the beginning. For older men, dating and courting are often synonymous. Their inability to handle a household and care adequately for themselves is a big factor that pushes them toward serious dating.

Men have other special problems, as Jane and Willard Kohn, co-authors of *The Widower*, tell us. Jane is professor of sociology at the University of Wisconsin, and Willard is the superintendent of a manufacturing plant. Both were widowed when they met while Jane was researching the plight of the widower. Both their book and their marriage grew out of that meeting. Willard speaks to the practical problems of the widower and Jane comments on the psychological, sociological, and physiological implications of his observations.

"Not only is this a paired society," wrote Willard, "but no clear-cut traditions or customs have been developed on how to behave toward the formerly married. A widower is perceived differently by different people. Many persons look at him as the debonair, man-about-town, a threat to women. Married women may see him as someone who is dying to make a pass at them."[1]

Not every widower has that experience. Willard Kohn observed: "Other men claim that they have been pursued constantly, particularly by divorced and widowed women. . . .

If women think they are the only ones who get propositions, they are very wrong!"[2]

Lance, an unusually successful businessman, found dating to be an unpleasant time. "I did not enjoy the dating process at all. What I found was that there was a real demand for short, fat, bald men fifty years old—especially for gentlemen who might have a decent standard of living. That really surprised me. It was a real ego boost. There are so many single women out there. There were all kinds of people wanting to line me up with dates. I couldn't handle it. Because I like people, I liked all the dates. I like everybody. I didn't want to hurt people ... but if you take them out the second time, well. ... It was a very unpleasant situation for me to get involved in."

The widow also may find herself in awkward situations. She may feel like a fifth wheel when included at a dinner party or other social function, even though her hostess is tactful and has the best of motives. Unfortunately, there are many insecure wives who feel threatened by single women. Not until the widow has fully recovered from her grief, established a new direction for her life, and accepted her singleness, will she and those around her feel more at ease.

Men are generally more comfortable with taking the initiative in dating. When I asked Larry whether he or his wife Evelyn had made the first contact, he answered quickly, "I did!" Then he described the situation: "First it was a letter acknowledging her loss, and an offer to talk, and letting her know I would like to see her and talk over old times. But I didn't push it. About a month later she called when she was in town. So we made a date and I took her to dinner where we chatted for about two hours."

For Neil and Emily, the dating process started differently. "We had gone to grammar school together when we were kids," said Neil. "She invited me over for dinner along with two other couples who had been long-time, mutual friends."

In today's social environment, it doesn't really matter who takes the initiative, as long as both people are comfortable with the arrangement.

Given that they aren't interested in high-tech dating, how do older widowed persons find each other? Where can they go to find security and openness? Remarried people I interviewed frequently mentioned social contact through a church. Sometimes they began dating people who had been friends or acquaintances for forty years or more. Many had friends in common who encouraged them to date each other.

Contact earlier in life was the second most common origin for dating. Many had known each other as children or teens, had been neighbors at one time, or were aware of each other in school. Only in a few instances were the spouses previously unknown to each other.

Among those who knew each other before they began dating, several renewed contact when they expressed concern for the loss of the other's spouse. Loren tells how it happened to him. "I called Esther up to thank her for her sympathy card and also asked her if she would be interested in going to the symphony with me. I had season tickets. I knew she was interested in music too. But she let me know right off the bat that this was a platonic relationship, that she was not interested in going with anybody. And I wasn't looking for a girlfriend, but I did want a companion to help ease me over the adjustment."

Some widowed persons resent arranged dates. David has

vivid memories of such an experience: "I was invited out to dinner at a lady's house. She was not interested in me herself, but she had invited another woman for me to complete three couples. I didn't feel like I wanted someone else telling me who to choose. I wanted to be the initiator and not have someone else arrange it for me."

FEAR OF DATING AGAIN

Many among the widowed are simply afraid to begin dating again. It can be a threatening experience, especially for women. One woman who conducts a grief therapy ministry commented on this in an interview: "The widowed are scared to come alive again, scared to move into the dating scene. I found this to be so myself, even though I was a very social creature. You lose your dating skills."

She warned that, particularly for those who are thirty-five to fifty years old, the promiscuity common in the general public spills over into the Christian social scene. The meat-market mentality that sees women as a commodity for men to enjoy lurks in the shadows. And some women pursue men by dressing seductively and flirting aggressively.

All of this is clearly out of bounds for Christians, who are responsible to order their lives according to biblical principles: "It is God's will that ... you should avoid sexual immorality; that each of you should learn to control his [or her] own body in a way that is holy and honorable, not in passionate lust like the heathen, who do not know God; and that in this matter no one should wrong his brother or take advantage of him" (1 Thessalonians 4:3–6).

One particularly valuable resource for any widowed

person is *Too Close, Too Soon,* by Jim Talley and Bobbie Reed. It fully addresses the dating process. While the book is written for a younger audience, many of its principles and warnings can be helpful for anyone. The book warns against the dangers of moving too quickly into emotional and physical intimacy during the dating process. Talley's relationship charts reveal clearly what too fast means. He believes that for a couple to spend three hundred hours alone over seven months or less may result in frustration, disappointment, or disaster.[3]

PLAYING IT SAFE THROUGH THE "NON-DATE"

In an article on dating for divorced persons, Jann Mitchell suggested that a safe emotional environment can be provided by the "non-date." The same idea can be used by the widowed.[4]

The case of Dr. Harry Westin and Eva, from chapter 1, illustrates the non-date from Harry's perspective. He thought that he and Eva were "just having dinner together." There was no thought of emotional entanglements, even after all those months. Several women I interviewed pointed to the same sort of thing when they spoke of keeping things on a platonic level. As long as both people agree on its importance, a safe emotional distance can be maintained through the non-date in several ways.

An agreement that each person will pay their own way at a restaurant is one way to set up a non-date. Neither person leaves the meal feeling that they owe anything to the other. Most men will object to this arrangement at first, especially if they are older. They are usually more serious in their dating and few of them are used to treating a date as a financial equal. Traveling separately to a restaurant will further decrease the risk of too much emotional involvement.

On any non-date, it helps to keep the conversation focused on the present, without any reference to what the future may bring. Find out what the other person is interested in and talk about those things. Try to find common ground and relate to each other as friends of the same sex. The non-date may kill the romantic notion of "love at first sight," but it will allow a genuine friendship to develop.

LET THE PHONE GROW OUT OF YOUR EAR

The telephone can be a valuable tool for controlling and improving your dating. It can be used both to maintain a safe distance and to draw people into deeper involvement. Those who examine Talley's book will find that he counts hours on the phone as part of the total by which he calculates the growing intimacy between a couple. Considering his young audience, that is wise. But not all the guidelines applicable to younger people necessarily fit seniors.

Seniors may be separated by distance or may have a physical disability that prevents frequent contact, except by phone. Some find it easier to reveal themselves over the phone. Norene, who had suffered through both a death and a divorce, was very cautious about socializing. "I preferred the telephone conversations," she said, "they were safer."

Convenience was a major reason for Eric and Angie's use of the phone. "Our friendship was on the telephone more than anything else," Angie told me. "We would talk for two to three hours a day. We got to calling mostly in the evenings because both of us are night people. Evenings are the hardest and longest time for people who are alone."

She remembered one particularly striking incident: "When I hung up one time after a late night call I thought, 'What did I say?' I had been on the phone for two-and-a-half hours. But it was in all this talking that we realized we both liked the same things." Eric added, "And we discovered more about our own personalities too, by just talking."

For Neil the phone played an important role in drawing him closer to Emily. "I'd never been with anyone in my life where we could just talk together," he said. "I took her out to dinner and we went to the beach a time or two. We went out with our friends and church group. I think what helped me more than anything was to be with Emily at the time of my loss and have somebody I could really talk to. . . . Every single morning either I called her at 6 A.M. or she called me. We knew the phone would ring."

So go ahead. Copy the teenagers. Let the phone grow out of your ear. You will discover common interests, learn important things about the other person and gain insight about yourself. It can also create a safer emotional environment for the early stages of dating. It could save you from a disastrous remarriage, and it may prepare you for smooth sailing into a happy future with a new partner!

What makes a winner in the dating game? It involves:

1. Allowing time to be at ease in singleness.
2. Thinking through your attitudes and standards again.
3. Determining your own unique strategy.
4. Overcoming the fear of new relationships.
5. Proceeding with caution.

3

Me? See a Counselor?

When I asked Roger and Nora why they didn't seek premarital counseling, Roger responded as many evangelical Christians might: "Well, when I started dating Nora I felt definitely led by the Lord. If I had such a leading as that, why would I need the counseling? That never occurred to me."

"I don't believe people of our age [late fifties when they were remarried] think of counseling," added Nora. "We know that's emphasized a lot now days, but it wasn't to people of our generation. We never heard of counseling when we were young."

Premarital counseling and other kinds of psychological therapy have become popular and widely available only in the last half of the twentieth century, so seniors are largely unacquainted with them. While extended counseling may be needed early in the grief recovery process and at certain other critical points during the adjustment to singleness, it is essential during the process of serious dating and immediately before marriage.

Roger and Nora gave us two reasons why some seniors are reluctant to seek counsel: They believe God's direct guidance is enough, and they are unfamiliar with the process and its benefits. Though they seem to have achieved a successful second marriage without counseling, some couples I talked to found the going very rough.

Others reject counseling because they feel age and experience are all they need. One person said, "Seeking counsel is a cop-out for people who are unwilling to make decisions."

These comments show what many Americans and most seniors think about counseling. Not only is the process of counseling a mystery to them, but they also wonder, "Why should I see a counselor?"

This was confirmed for me by the written questionnaires returned from six states.[1] Only 7 percent of seniors said they had received premarital counseling. Of those who did not, 88 percent said they saw no need for it, and 12 percent were skeptical about the process. While widowed persons who remarry experience nothing like the 40 to 60 percent failure rate that is typical for divorced people who remarry, their marriages can still come apart.[2]

In fairness, it needs to be said there are some older widowed persons who are open to help through counseling and recognize its value. Larry, one of those with a positive view of counseling, commented: "When you grow older and have lived with a mate, you're set in your ways. Then you're in with another mate and she has different ways. You've got to adjust. Sometimes it's hard. You run into difficulties. Then you should be counseled on such things."

The reasons a person seeks counseling vary. Norene wanted to regain wholeness and to feel better about herself. Evelyn was trying to get past a feeling of betraying her first husband. "I felt kind of guilty at the time because I thought people would look down on me for not waiting at least a year or more [to get married]," she explained. "I thought if my first husband knew about it, he'd feel I sure didn't think much of him to go ahead and marry so quickly."

A widowed person living alone has the option of seeking help or postponing it indefinitely. But because many younger widowed persons are trying to hold their families together, they can't afford to delay counseling.

YOUNGER WIDOWED PERSONS
KNOW THEY NEED HELP

Younger widowed persons with children at home can face terrible situations, where they know their lives will explode unless they get help. Lisa was left with a small boy to care for when her husband died. "I went to a counselor with my son," she said. "He had a lot of trouble with the loss. He became depressed . . . didn't want to go to school . . . was afraid he would lose me. I had to start taking him to school, otherwise he wouldn't leave the house."

When a young father is taken from a home, a boy especially has trouble. He has lost his role model, someone who gives him his basic identity in life. One mother told me of a frightening experience when her young son came into the room threatening to harm himself. His exact words were, "Maybe I should just go see my dad and end all this."

Another widow with a small boy said he was so distraught after his dad died that he became suicidal. He tried to run out in front of cars and even jumped from the second floor of their house. He couldn't understand why his dad would leave him after promising to teach him how to fish and to play baseball. Such behaviors are cries for help, and they can't be ignored.

The future partner for the widowed person with teens or young children may be a person who has never married or is divorced or widowed. This person may not have children. Counseling for everyone involved in this new family relationship is strongly recommended. It helps if that process can begin early in courtship and continue through to both premarital and post marital issues. Many find this essential for survival of their marriages.

REASONS TO SEEK COUNSEL

Regardless of your age or personal views on counseling, there are important reasons for every widowed person to seek counseling before remarriage. Let's look at three major ones.

The need to gain objectivity. To understand ourselves, to be able to step outside ourselves and our feelings for a moment and really see what is going on in our lives, that is the gift an objective counselor can give us. The Scottish poet Robert Burns put it this way: "O the gift to see ourselves as others see us." As we receive this gift, we will see our circumstances more clearly.

Good counselors can help us see the other people in our lives more realistically. Sometimes, they can help us see and avoid traps that were invisible to us. Christian therapists can also keep us from misreading either the Bible or providential directions.

Some of us prefer to share our struggles only with friends and family. But will they tell us the truth? Are they able to? They may be too close to our pain to see clearly. They may not want to disagree with us and cause more pain. So they tell us only what we hope to hear.

It's becoming a requirement of churches. A second reason to seek premarital counseling is that an increasing number of churches or pastors are making it a requirement. It's always possible to escape to a Las Vegas style wedding chapel, a justice of the peace or a less demanding minister. Couples who do this often have deep regrets for the rest of their lives because of the things they could have avoided through good counseling.

David told me his church required six weeks of counseling, either in a group setting or as a couple. Though he didn't particularly feel the need for counseling, he was wise enough to see there was more he could learn. "I wanted to find out what their thinking was and to see if I was still missing something," he said.

David's wife, Norene, added: "I welcomed it. I wanted it. I needed some self-affirmation, to know that I was okay and wasn't going to have another failure."

One California church has created an interlocking series of programs that support the widowed. When people lose a spouse, they are strongly encouraged to be part of an organized support group. It meets monthly. They are asked to continue in that group for up to two years as needed. This group aids in grief recovery and provides the widowed with input from others with similar experiences. When the time comes for remarriage, this church requires one Sunday session a week for sixteen weeks in a premarital counseling class.

It *helps you evaluate motives*. A third reason for counseling is to help evaluate our real motives for remarrying. A badly motivated remarriage can lead to disappointment or disaster. A man may only be looking for a care giver to help him in his later years. A women who is not financially independent may be desperately searching for a man to provide her with security. Some men want a housekeeper and cook, while some women really just want a gardener or someone who can make house repairs. Anyone may be desperately lonely and just want another body in the house.

Those seniors responding to my questionnaire were able to acknowledge some of their real motives for marrying. Eighty-nine percent listed loneliness as having "some" or "great" influence on their decision. Sexual fulfillment was named by 59 percent as having "great" or "some" influence on their pursuit of a mate. "Great" or "some" emotional needs, such as love, sent 96 percent on a search for an understanding companion.

All of these desires may be fulfilled as a by-product of a healthy marriage. If they are the primary motive for getting married, however, they will probably create problems. Usually, outside counseling is needed to resolve such problems.

Since most people have not had prior experience with the counseling process, they have lots of questions about it. What kind of counselor should I see? What will it cost? How long will it take? Where can I find the help I need? What happens in a counseling session?

WHAT KIND OF COUNSELOR?

Most of us who are facing the long recovery from personal tragedy or are looking for guidance about remarriage, will not need to see a psychiatrist. These medically trained professionals usually handle much more severe problems than we will face. Sometimes they are called in to help the widowed with the special medical problems associated with severe depression. But for short-term and long-term therapy where medication and medical testing are not part of the treatment, a psychologist or other non-medical professional will usually be the best choice.

Look for a certified or licensed counselor. Counselors should be members in good standing of the American Psychological Association, the American Psychiatric Association or a similar professional group. Either the national or state organization should have some information on anyone you are considering. Keep in mind, however, that some competent and licensed therapists may choose not to belong to a particular professional body for personal reasons.

Most states have a certification agency which allows counselors to call themselves psychologists. In some states the title *counselor* when used professionally is controlled by a public agency too. Licensing is also required to use the names *marriage and family counselor* or *social worker* professionally.

Select a counselor sympathetic to your faith. It is very important for Christians that a counselor be sympathetic to their faith.

This means they should have a basic commitment to the Bible as a legitimate source of inspiration and authority. Whoever you see, it is best to get a recommendation from some knowledgeable, spiritually mature person who you trust. If possible, it is good to talk to a former client of the counselor.

Many seminaries now sponsor or are connected with counseling centers and provide referral services for those looking for help. A quick check of the Yellow Pages for my city also revealed five groups of counselors openly identifying themselves as Christian. Individual counselors who are believers can also be identified by knowledgeable Christian leaders.

Find a counselor you're comfortable with. Selecting a counselor is like selecting a physician. You must be comfortable with the person and have confidence in them. A person does not have to stay with the first counselor he or she visits. Shopping around is a normal part of the selection process. Some people interview two or three therapists and then select the one they think can help them most. Once a satisfactory person has been found, however, it is best to stay with that counselor until some progress has been made.

Look at what is available in your church. If a person's counseling needs are not complicated by problems requiring long-term help, the resources of a local church can often meet the need. Pastors, pastor-counselors or trained lay counselors are normally available to work with both church members and other people seeking assistance.

If there is a licensed professional counselor on the church staff or a counselor works with the staff on a referral basis, fees will usually be charged. In most situations, a person's own church or a larger one nearby is the first place to look for help. This is one place where your faith will be respected and biblical principles will be carefully applied in the counseling process.

Check out the costs. Hourly rates for professional counselors vary widely, so it is impractical to quote any dollar figures here. For many people, the cost can be quite high. Because of this, many private counselors and clinics have a sliding fee scale, adjusted to the counselee's ability to pay. For those with lower incomes, some help is available from public agencies. Other people have partial insurance coverage for counseling services through their employer's group policy. Even some non-group policies now cover limited amounts of counseling.

The total length of time in counseling will certainly affect the final cost, and it may vary greatly. The time involved may be an hour a week for a few weeks or a few months, depending on the purpose and the progress. Unless arrangements can be made for the insurance company to make payment directly to the counselor, payment is expected at the end of each session.

THE COUNSELING PROCESS

There is nothing mysterious about a counseling session. Professional counselors are part of the helping professions. They strive to be supportive listeners who guide counselees toward positive solutions. Some take a more directive approach than others, but they are not usually advice givers who tell a person what to do.

The individual or couple seeking help may feel nervous

during the first interview, but with a capable counselor this feeling usually disappears quickly. You may go to a counselor for help with any aspect of life. Counselors are sensitive people and will endeavor to put you at ease and be supportive throughout the sessions.

Complete honesty and openness on the part of the counselee is important to gain good results from counseling sessions. This is a time for you to talk about hurts, feelings, dreams, problems, hopes, or anything else related to the purpose of your visit. In premarital counseling some tests may be given to help you and your future spouse gain insight into your personalities and evaluate your compatibility.

A FINAL CAUTION

Counseling is an intense learning experience, and one of the greatest obstacles to getting help is a know-it-all attitude. Older people sometimes make the mistake of saying, "I've lived this long, so I have all the answers."

Even with the younger widowed there may be problems. "I've been married, so I have experience," they may say. "What can you tell me?" Such people need to remember that grieving and adjusting to singleness have changed them and that their new relationship will never be the same as any previous one.

Men and women do not automatically profit by their past experience; neither age nor professional status guarantees success in marriage. As one professional acknowledged, "Some of the most traumatic, painful divorces are experienced by professionals such as myself—psychiatrists, psychologists, counselors, and social workers."[3]

This reality should not keep a person from seeking counsel from professionals, but it sharply reminds us that everyone needs help from others at some time. As the saying warns, "He who has himself as his lawyer, has a fool for a client."

Whether you choose to rely on church counseling resources or seek out professionals in private practice, working with a competent counselor can make the difference between success or failure when romance blooms again.

A SUMMARY OF COUNSELING

1. Counseling helps us to gain objectivity, meet church requirements, and evaluate our motives for marrying.

2. In evaluating counselors not serving at my church I need to know if they are:

- State licensed.
- Not hostile to my faith.
- Recommended by a trusted spiritual leader or friend.
- Someone with whom I feel comfortable.

3. The counseling process works well only for those who are completely open and honest.

4

Courting and Deciding

Time magazine in an April 24, 1989, article on modern life and its unusual pressures commented: "The necessities of time are also out of reach. . . . Even mourning time. In 1922 Emily Post instructed that the proper mourning period for a mature widow was three years. Fifty years later Amy Vanderbilt urged that the bereaved be about their normal business within a week or so."[1]

If Amy Vanderbilt meant some day-to-day activities by *normal business*, then her advice is understandable. But the normal grieving process takes much longer than one week. Only after it is finished are the widowed ready for either social dating or courtship, which is often an extension of dating.

HOW LONG SHOULD I WAIT?

The issue of courtship raises a new concern: If friendship, dating and courting are leading toward remarriage, how long should the widowed wait to remarry?

Some remarried couples say that the length of a courtship can vary greatly because of the differences in each couple's circumstances. They may have known each other for many years, and the extra time retirement makes available for courting can move the relationship along more quickly. Some point to the limited time many older widowed persons have before death as a justification for quick remarriage.

However, all the professional counselors I interviewed, including pastors, psychologists, and lay counselors, strongly suggested waiting for at least a year after a death or divorce before remarriage. Some insisted that this criteria should apply to all the widowed, no matter what their circumstances. One reason for this position is the great number of failed marriages any counselor sees.

A second reason for the widowed to wait is that grieving takes more time than many people realize. Objective judgment can be impaired and decisions later regretted. Cutting short the waiting time not only hurts the one who is impatient, but it can also damage the new marriage.

One minister to senior adults will not remarry anyone who refuses to wait a year after their loss. He prefers that any widowed person wait a year even to date and doubts that any other significant decision should be made before that time has passed. I asked him if he shows mercy to those who are seventy-five or eighty years old and realize they have little time left. He answered, "No, we don't want to give the impression we are encouraging them to rush into something, even at advanced age."

This pastor has the full support of a large and loyal congregation who have gone out of their way to create a diverse and supportive ministry to all the widowed. There is a long-term grief therapy group and a sixteen-week Sunday school class for engaged couples, which is required for anyone wishing to be married in the church. "We put [the widowed who are remarrying] through as much preparation as we do the divorced," this pastor observed. In his congregation, he is likely to get a very cooperative response.

Such definite timetables and highly structured environments are not the only response to the remarriage of the widowed. When asked about quick remarriage among the older widowed, a pastor in another church replied, "I'd say, 'Go for it!' " He did not mean that caution should be cast aside or good counsel ignored, but that extenuating circumstances should be considered and any tendency toward legalism should be softened.

When Yorty and Anna were remarried at age seventy-five, their pastor was similarly lenient. After Anna informed him about how things were developing with Yorty and that they had known each other since childhood, he told her: "Anna, you're not getting any younger. You'd better do what you're going to do and do it quickly!"

A third reason to wait is that long-established standards of etiquette have dictated that one year is the proper waiting period for remarriage.

Some individuals still feel this social pressure. Ed told me about his situation with Tammy: "She was ready to get married. But I was afraid 'they' would look down on me if I remarried in less than a year, so we waited a year and a few days and then got married."

Sometimes, traditions from the past can trap us in a kind of societal legalism. When there is any period of waiting, no matter what the cause, the reasons for it should be discussed ahead of time, clearly understood and mutually agreed upon.

CAN SPECIAL CIRCUMSTANCES CHANGE THE WAITING PERIOD?

Obviously, not all counselors agree on how long to wait before remarrying or how to weigh special circumstances. Here are some questions to consider when trying to establish more flexible policies for remarriage. Many counselors agree that positive answers to more than one of these questions justifies an early remarriage.

1. Is the couple quite elderly?
2. Did they lose their previous spouses through process deaths (as opposed to sudden deaths), and is there evidence that much of the grieving process took place as the eventual death was approaching?
3. Have the two considering remarriage known each other most of their lives?
4. Has the couple submitted to counseling and are all other remarriage guidelines fulfilled?

Rushing into another relationship for the wrong reasons is dangerous and unfair for both people. So the word is, wait! Wait for healing. Wait for clear perspective. Wait for direction and wisdom from above. Any exception to the one-year waiting period should be made only after careful reflection and wise counsel.

SHORT COURTSHIP, STRAINED MARRIAGE

One remarried wife was adamant about what she would have changed in her courtship. "I wouldn't let a possible mate rush me into marriage in five months. He said our age prompted it and I had already accepted." This wife was seventy-seven when she remarried, and her husband was past eighty years of age.

She added, "It has worked out, but each person should have more time to try to be somewhat sure they will be fair by not mentally measuring one's ways and habits so strongly against a former mate." In her case a brief courtship that cut discussion time too short added greatly to the strain of remarriage.

When relatively short amounts of time (less than a year) elapse between the loss of a mate, renewed courting, and remarriage, unexpected issues often surface. Wrong choices may be made, and unresolved grief can carry over into the new marriage. The new mate may be expected to solve all kinds of problems associated with loneliness or other unresolved feelings. There may even be lingering doubts about what others may think.

A BRIEF COURTSHIP THAT SUCCEEDED

Neil, who was personally involved in the care of his first wife during her long final illness, had this to say about his wait of only four months before remarriage. "That was one of the things I really felt guilty about afterwards, because I remarried in such a short time. Beforehand, I was afraid of what my children would think, and afterward what my friends would think.

"However, after Jenny died I determined I was not going to just stay at home. I went to church activities and so forth. I remember two different occasions when I went to church dinners and sat across from our friends of many years. Twice I got up and left because I couldn't take it being alone with the other couples. I still feel that the Lord brought Emily along for me at just the right time."

While such a short courtship is not recommended, Neil and Emily's successful remarriage is something for which they are grateful to God. Its success was helped by their friendship over many years, Emily's good relationship with Neil's previous spouse, and their commitments to God and each other.

It was also helped because it followed a process death, where Neil was the major care giver for his terminally ill wife over a long period. During the course of a terminal illness, much of the widowed person's grieving is completed.

The individual also has ample opportunity to think about the future, often with assistance from the dying spouse. Sometimes the dying mate talks specifically about the possibility of remarriage for the survivor. Some spouses even made definite suggestions for their replacement. One actually made a list!

SOME MAKE HASTE SLOWLY

In stark contrast to the previous example, Roger and Nora had an unusually long courtship: four-and-a-half years.

This happened even though they had known each other for nearly forty years, lived in the same community, and attended the same church. Roger was widowed over two years before Nora, but he came to date her only a month after her loss.

"I informed him it would be platonic," Nora explained, "which it was for quite a while. He had season tickets to the symphony so we went there and to dinner on Friday nights at the end of the work week. It took me a long time to transfer my love from one man to another. A man transfers his love more easily, I think."

Lisa, age thirty-six when she was widowed, waited two-and-a-half years before remarrying. She took that long even though she and her ailing first husband grieved together and talked about her life after he was gone. He didn't want her to live alone and encouraged her to begin dating early.

"I was determined not to do anything or make any big decisions for the first year," Lisa said. "I had to get through all the anniversary times and special holidays like Christmas, and I wasn't ready emotionally. It was a year and a half after I started dating Darryl before we married; there were too many complications with both of us having two children at home. Even so, it was scary when we both began to seriously consider it."

MAKING CHOICES

Whether the widowed are consciously looking or are determined they will never remarry, they need to socialize. So who do they look for as a friend of the other sex?

One eighty-seven-year-old senior I interviewed surprised

me with her requirements for a mate. Dressed regally in a tailored, knitted dress with strands of pearls around her neck, she talked with me in her tastefully furnished apartment in a high-rise retirement center. Despite having been a battered wife, Isabel maintained a sense of humor. She had been divorced after a traumatic first marriage and then widowed twice.

With rolling, bouncy laughter she told me of her partial list of what she had wanted in a man after that first failed marriage. "I wanted a man with his own teeth and hair, and with no [protruding] stomach."

There is one universally disastrous motive for dating and courting. As one person put it: "If a person is interested in another just to have someone to go to bed with, forget it. That's a dead-end street."

When choosing a new marriage partner, there are certain questions that must be settled without emotional confusion or unrealistic time pressures. They have to do with our value system and those things that are most important in our lives. We must finally decide who or what guides our thinking and decision making processes. For a committed Christian, the question must include an examination of our spiritual disciplines and basic commitment to Christ. We need to be sure that the believers we are spending time with help us clarify and uphold these values. Any potential spouse should certainly share, strengthen, and expand our moral and spiritual values.

Many of those interviewed held strong convictions about what kinds of moral and spiritual values they wanted a mate to possess. Eric said, "One of my requirements was that she had to be of the same faith. I met a lot of people on trips with a non-church retirement group, but they had habits like gambling and so on that I didn't care for. So it was at church that we met. Angie was someone I knew, not a complete stranger to me."

Nancy put it this way: "It's so very important to have similar backgrounds, similar interests. But having the Lord is number one. He is the center of our lives."

When Loren and Esther began dating, the issue of commitment to Christ was of central importance. "One of the first things I asked her," said Loren, "was how important Jesus Christ was in her life. She hesitated a moment, thought about it and said, 'Well, Loren, he's the most important one in my life.'

"I thought, 'That does it! I'm not looking any farther for a girl.' I didn't want to go with someone who was casually interested in the Lord. I attribute the success of our marriage to the fact that when we decided to get married, we asked the Lord to make himself the center of our home, and he has. This really works."

Neil agreed with those sentiments: "I would never have married someone if I had any doubts whatsoever about their integrity and everything about them. And if Emily hadn't been a Christian who really loved the Lord and put him first in her life, well . . ."

Some people were totally organized and very goal oriented as they evaluated and pursued the courting process. Lance, the successful businessman, took a Hawaiian vacation after the sudden loss of his wife. There he began thinking about the future. He made a list of what he was looking for in a wife as well as a list of prospects. He began dating within two months after being widowed. He admits coming close to a bad marriage before finding his new wife, Rana.

Interestingly enough, Rana was not a list maker, but she still had definite standards for a mate. "I wanted someone who cared about family, who was a Christian, and a sensitive person." With a bright smile she added, "Lance has filled the bill!"

Though the remarried were looking for many different things in a new mate, three characteristics appeared repeatedly. The first was a deep love for Christ. A complete picture of the other person's past and present was also important. Finally, mutual interests, which offer the possibility of companionship and compatibility, were a high priority.

DON'T MARRY WITHOUT IT!

Anyone who has spent much time in church has heard about the three Greek words for love. All three need to be part of any marriage or remarriage. *Philos* means friendship and has to do with the comfort we feel in another's presence. Any couple who can say, "He [or she] is my best friend," is very fortunate. These kinds of couples can work well together and will enjoy each other's companionship.

Agape has to do more with commitment than comfort and is really a function of the will. It speaks of loving in the face of rejection or wounds and calls us to act in the other's best interest.

Eros is what we often see at the movies and on television. It has to do more with sexual and sensual attraction. While this classical Greek word does not appear in the Bible, its idea of passion, joy, and fulfillment in marriage certainly does.[2]

Many of the widowed are mystified by the intensity of their new love. Sometimes it frightens them. They didn't realize it was possible for a second love to be deeper than the first one they had known for so long. They were often caught off guard by an intense physical attraction and emotional highs.

One widow, who affirmed her complete love for her first husband and satisfaction with her first marriage, said: "So it was a complete surprise and somewhat disconcerting when I found myself so quickly and completely smitten by Jim. I found myself reacting just like a teenager [she remarried at age fifty-five], and I couldn't believe it. I thought I had more sense! It was a difficult time for a while to adjust to my feelings. . . . I had to make a conscious decision to be objective."

Being surprised by passion in a new love makes objectivity difficult, but that widow was wise to recognize the need. It helped her make the tough decisions for her immediate future.

In the following chapters, we'll look at some critical issues which need to be faced when the widowed decide to remarry.

BEFORE REMARRYING, THE WIDOWED MUST. . .

1. Have completed the grieving process.
2. Feel truly single again and be totally committed to the Lord's will for singleness or marriage.

3. Have a mutually agreed upon dating and courting process.
4. Have separated right from wrong motives in dating and remarrying.
5. Complete any needed or required counseling.

5

Protecting Your Assets

"The road to hell," it is said, "is paved with good intentions." Simply trusting in someone's good intentions when it comes to financial matters may lead down the bumpy road to financial chaos or ruin. A genuine biblical perspective calls for us to be responsible managers of all we have. This is evident both from the example of Adam as a caretaker in the garden and from the parables of Jesus about the prodigal son and the rich fool.

While honesty and integrity are important in addressing financial issues, they alone will not help us sort out our legal and financial lives. Unless a couple's assets amount to little more than their monthly Social Security income, advice from a trusted attorney, financial counselor, or accountant can provide needed guidance with these details of remarriage. When there are property holdings, business ventures, stocks, bonds, debts, or other complex elements involved, this advice is essential.

ASK QUESTIONS, EXPECT ANSWERS

Before remarriage, all couples need to have a "no holds barred" question and answer time about their individual and joint financial conditions. A marriage of trust is easier to build if there is full understanding in advance. Here are some questions to help guide a couple's private discussions or prepare them for a meeting with a professional:

What resources are you each bringing to the marriage? Are there any savings accounts or insurance coverage? What kinds of real property will be part of the new estate? Be prepared to give a detailed list of your assets.

Will your assets be pooled, held jointly, or both? If one of you owns a home and both of you move into it, will the other partner become a joint owner of the property? If not, where will the surviving spouse live if the homeowner dies? How might the disposition of other assets be affected by an unexpected death?

If there is a great difference in the resources you each bring to the marriage, how will that affect the relationship? Will either of you change your lifestyle significantly because of the remarriage?

WHEN QUESTIONS ARE NOT ASKED

In spite of the importance of financial planning, many couples do not discuss these issues before they get married.

"I didn't know if Larry had a lot of money or no money at

all!" Evelyn recalled. "I don't think either one of us said anything about it."

Larry added, "We figured it was nobody's business!"

"Well, it should have been each other's business," Evelyn interjected. "It didn't dawn on us to ask any questions."

Fortunately, Larry and Evelyn had known each other for many years and had a common basis for trust. They are still together and doing well. In their case, lack of communication about finances during courtship did not destroy the marriage.

But another "no questions asked" courtship didn't turn out so well. I interviewed the daughter of a widow who almost lost everything. Her mother's story illustrates how important it is to get all the facts and how seductive a con artist can be.

Lucille sold the suburban mini-farm she and her deceased husband owned and bought a modest home in town. When the transaction was complete, she had less than $10,000 left. To supplement her Social Security income, she cared for an older woman who was dying.

She had been hired for this job by the woman's handsome son, Dan. Both before and after his mother's death, Dan and Lucille dated, but Lucille resisted his pressure to remarry quickly.

It soon became necessary for Dan to have back surgery. After he was released from the hospital, Lucille invited him to stay at her house so she could care for him. She was happy to be needed and loved to cook big meals for him. He didn't hurry his recovery.

During his recovery, Dan was very affectionate toward her. Lucille had missed this kind of attention since her husband had died, and it made her all the more vulnerable to Dan's developing trap.

After about six months, Dan persuaded Lucille to marry him. From the very beginning of their marriage, he tried to get her to put her house in his name or at least to make them co-owners. Fortunately, Lucille remembered her first husband saying many times, only half jokingly, "Oh, when I die, you'll just let some guy come along and take all your money away from you."

When Dan had spent much of Lucille's money and she still stubbornly refused to sign the house over to him, he became angry. Finally, at her urging, he moved out of the house, saying, "Well, I was just getting ready to leave you anyhow, because you don't have any more money left in your bank account."

Later Lucille learned that Dan had married several widows before her. When their bank accounts were used up or if he had persuaded them to sign their houses over to him, he would leave.

Lucille saw too late that she should have done some things differently. She had missed some clear warning signs. She had not known Dan for very long before they were married, and he was rather close-mouthed about his past. She had asked few questions about his resources, values or plans for the future. When she did ask, his answers were always general and uninformative.

She had been too lonely to recognize Dan's slow recovery as a ploy to work on her sympathy and gain power over her. When they were married, she had allowed Dan to whisk her away to another city where they exchanged their vows before a Justice of the Peace. Lucille hadn't even talked with her children or a pastor about it beforehand. She had never thought to discuss her finances with anyone.

WARNING SIGNS

The American Bar Association and the Attorney General's Criminal Justice Division Financial Fraud Office do not have statistics on the number of widows or widowers who are victims of this kind of fraud. Most such experiences go unreported; the embarrassment is just too great.

Here are some signs that point to potential danger:

1. The intended victim has little or no personal information on their suitor's background and he or she seems to have no friends or family who can provide such information.
2. The pursuer provides overwhelming emotional support, through physical affection and subtle flattery.
3. The victim does not have close family nearby or does not confide in them until too late.
4. The pursuer wants an early marriage, "So I can take care of you" or "So we can be together."
5. The victimizer suggests a simple, private, and speedy wedding, often in a nearby state which has less restrictive marriage license requirements and no waiting period.
6. The victimizer claims to have great financial resources which are tied up for some reason.
7. After the marriage, the emotional support, compliments, and affection drop precipitously.
8. Sudden financial reverses are claimed by the victim-

izer soon after the marriage and requests for financial help begin.

9. The victimizer is very persistent about putting his or her name on property deeds and bank accounts.
10. If the victim does not consult an attorney by this time, he or she has entered the trap.

The story of Lucille and Dan may help others thinking of remarriage by reminding them to ask probing questions and get verifiable answers.

WOULD A PREMARITAL AGREEMENT HELP?

A prenuptial agreement may help you avoid both outright deception and simple misunderstandings. One out of five people responding to my survey said they had sought legal advice and had established a premarital contract regarding finances, property, or distribution of assets to children. Others realized they were headed for problems in their financial lives soon after marriage and had sought professional help to avoid them. A few who had problems later on said an agreement would have helped them.

The terms *premarital, prenuptial,* and *antenuptial* are used interchangeably. The American Bar Association's Public Education Division has a booklet entitled *Your Legal Guide To Marriage,* which covers prenuptial agreements along with many other topics.[1] It is well worth buying, but the information in it should not be used without further advice from a professional.

Prenuptial agreements were once only for the wealthy, but now any of us may find them useful. Women especially have more assets than they once did. Many of them have spent a lifetime working at a career, or they may be bringing the assets from a widow's inheritance into a new marriage.

The price of asset protection is not beyond the means of most of us. *Money* magazine reported, "Total legal fees run from $500 to several thousand dollars, depending on the complexity of the contract."[2]

In my interviews, I found only one instance where an attorney did not recommend a prenuptial agreement. Erin and Edna were a couple who had been neighbors in the same retirement center. The attorney suggested that they solve their financial problems the easy way, by just moving in together. Though they knew this was being done, it definitely wasn't for them. Obviously, when any professional's advice runs counter to a couple's moral convictions, they need to make an independent decision. Better yet, they should find a professional who shares their convictions.

FULL DISCLOSURE: THE ONLY WAY

In contrast to the couples who were silent about finances, Esther and Loren acted deliberately. "He came over one day with a list of all his assets," Esther explained. "He showed me this list and informed me he was well able to take care of me. Loren said, 'I imagine you own this home.' And I answered, 'Yes, I do.' But I didn't give him one bit of information at that point. I wasn't ready to."

By the time Esther and Loren were ready to marry, she had fully disclosed her financial status which included much more than the house.

As Loren put it: "Esther and I have a very smooth

relationship. One of the areas we have been very sensitive about has been our children and grandchildren. Right away we established a prenuptial agreement. We didn't do that to protect ourselves, but so that our children would feel comfortable regarding anything we might have and wouldn't worry about losing out. They might not say it, but we have noticed that it can be disastrous in a family if someone seems to be getting the inside track at the expense of others. So all our children [each have three] are aware of this prenuptial agreement."

When Bert and Elsie discussed their assets and liabilities before they married, they discovered that they were each in about the same financial situation. As soon as they were married, they made out new wills and each named the oldest son from their previous marriage as executor of their individual wills.

With the help of an attorney, they put everything into community property. The wills are totally reciprocal except for certain specified household items. The children were allowed to specify in writing what they wanted. Their selections were either given to them immediately, or reserved for them in the wills.

Wills are not the only financial area where planning is important. For couples like Bert and Elsie or Loren and Esther, who own their own homes before marriage, there is an important tax issue to consider. Couples who are age fifty-five or older should discuss their strategy for using the $125,000 capital-gains exclusion on the sale of their homes.

An article in *Money* magazine discussed the promises and pitfalls of this tax break: "Married couples, however, can take advantage of this tax break only once, even if they both own homes. As a result, you and your future spouse may be able to slash your tax bill significantly by selling both your abodes *before* you marry. Bear in mind that if you've already used your exclusion but your new spouse hasn't, he or she won't qualify for the tax break *after* you marry" (italics mine).[3]

An interesting twist to the housing issue came out in my interview with Darryl and Lisa. When they were married, Darryl moved into Lisa's house which she kept in her name on her lawyer's advice. While she may now change that, having the house and her own checking account give her a great feeling of security.

"I don't think I would ever be so dependent on a man again," Lisa explained. "I will always have my own resources. I may have to be on my own again sometime."

Lisa was not reflecting distrust, but the spirit of many younger women who work outside the home, handle their own finances, and recognize the fragility of life.

Some people think legal premarital agreements torpedo trust in a marriage, so they won't even consider one. However, one widow who remarried in her late forties commented, "It still sounds mercenary to me, but an understanding or prenuptial agreement regarding finances would have helped a lot. My husband still refuses to make out a will because he wants our money to go to his children. I continued to work for eight years, with almost as much salary as his, and later drew almost as much Social Security. But because I had no assets to bring to the marriage, he doesn't feel I am entitled to share equally with the children. This is still a problem, though I haven't pressed the issue."

Some of those interviewed felt that they took care of inheritance problems through their separate wills. However, it should be noted that states vary in their laws and may require certain provisions for the spouse if not covered properly in the will. It's wise to seek legal counsel.

When I asked Roger and Nora, who remarried in their late fifties, if they had drawn up a prenuptial agreement, Roger said, "No, . . . we sold our properties and together bought this place."

Nora volunteered, "I had a lot more [financial resources] than Roger had." When I asked how they settled things in merging their lives and resources, they jointly answered, "It's ours." Roger said, "What's mine is hers, what's hers is mine." Then Nora added, "We have never had things separate. Our names are on everything jointly. We have identical wills. Our checking account is one." Roger and Nora have been married many years now.

WILL YOU PAY YOUR NEW SPOUSE'S PREVIOUS DEBTS?

In general, the greater the financial resources brought to a marriage, the more often a couple signs legal, premarital agreements. An agreement is also a good safeguard when one partner brings large debts into a marriage. If the spouse with the debt died soon after the marriage, the other partner could face financial disaster.

However, an informal, non-legal agreement regarding debts does work for some people. When I asked David and Carolyn if they had a premarital agreement, David said: "No. I had some outstanding debts from business reversals so we kept things separate until we made arrangements to take care of them. After that, we put our accounts together. We did get some financial advice to make sure we weren't getting into something that could be detrimental to either one of us."

Carolyn added, "I kept what was mine in my name for a while. It wasn't until after two years that we finally put his name on the last of the accounts. And that helped me trust him."

PRECAUTIONS REGARDING PRENUPTIAL AGREEMENTS

If a couple decides to use a prenuptial agreement, there are certain cautions to be noted. Fairness aside, if there is not full disclosure of all income and assets as well as liabilities and obligations, the agreement may not stand up in court. Secondly, if the parties are not each represented by their own attorneys, proof of having freely entered into the agreement may be difficult to show, should there be need. As with any legal document, a prenuptial agreement should not be signed without fully understanding its contents.

Almost anything can be put into an agreement, but not all things are enforceable by law. You could specify who is to take out the trash or wash the dishes, but such seemingly frivolous items are not legally binding as in the case of real property or other investments. Putting some details into writing, whether binding or not, can help a couple work through their individual and joint concepts of day-to-day married life. Questions couples neglect to resolve before marriage are generally the ones that create serious conflict later on. The key words for financial and other aspects of marriage are always *open communication.*

WHAT ABOUT OTHER LEGAL INSTRUMENTS?

Durable power of attorney and *living trust* are other instruments intended to protect assets and provide for their proper administration. These function in the extremely difficult situation of a temporary or permanent disability, whether mental or physical.

If the disabled spouse is no longer capable of making decisions, giving directions, or perhaps even signing documents, who will legally do so on his or her behalf? A will is activated upon a death. But there are pre-death events which a will cannot help. When the crisis occurs, it may be too late to accomplish what the person would have wanted. Therefore, providing for such crises before they occur can greatly reduce their trauma.

To set up a durable power of attorney or living trust calls for total confidence between a husband and wife if they function as trustees. An alternate choice is to have an institution handle everything.

General information on the purpose of durable power of attorney or other options is available through the American Association of Retired Persons.[4] For complete information and specific advice, consult your attorney.

DISCUSS BURIAL PLANS BEFORE MARRIAGE?

Not necessarily. But for older couples with grown children, this may not be so farfetched. It may or may not have anything to do with finances. Yet the question will arise in the marriage and require an answer. Sometimes one or both parties have made investments in family plots long before the new marriage. What will be done with the unused sites? How will the newly wedded couple handle previous plans made with others? Who will be buried beside whom?

Roger and Nora made their plans in keeping with their pattern of sharing everything. "We have a plot together," they explained. "We started a new union and it's 'us' from here on."

Another couple who both had children from a previous marriage toyed with the idea of burial together. The wife recalled, "As time went on we decided that for our children's sake we would have the [biological] parents buried together. So he will be buried next to his first wife and I'll be buried next to my first husband."

Her husband added: "We feel that it is the children we should be concerned about rather than ourselves. Because, being gone, what do we care? But our children would want to visit their mother and dad together."

The wife explained, "Every Memorial Day our families visit the graves . . . but that's about the only time we go. To me that grave is empty. The person isn't there. We do it just as a form."

Most of the older couples interviewed had chosen to be buried with a previous mate. This reflected economic factors, consideration for their children, or other personal motives.

When she married a twice-widowed man who had not served in the military, one widow lost her right to be buried without charge in the veteran's cemetery beside her first husband. While she will not be buried near either of her husbands, she says she is ". . . perfectly satisfied for him [her present spouse] to be buried by his second wife. Some people are sensitive about those things. It's good we have discussed them."

Discussing final plans need not be a macabre or somber business. By handling serious questions sensibly, mature couples can move into a new marriage with fewer shadows and more laughter.

HERE'S WHAT WE'VE DISCOVERED:

1. Ask pointed questions about each other's resources prior to the wedding; expect and give satisfying answers.
2. Give and expect full financial disclosure.
3. Consider carefully your possible need for a prenuptial agreement.
4. Be aware of other legal instruments, such as durable power of attorney.
5. Be prepared to talk about that "final" investment: burial plans.

6

Money, Money, Money

In every remarriage there are habits, ways of thinking, and opinions shaped by the previous years and relationships. Those attitudes that relate to money are always sensitive issues. A courting couple can begin to test their compatibility in this area by first taking an internal audit of their own attitudes toward money. The following questions will help them examine themselves and formulate questions for discussion:

What is your attitude toward money? Is it a consuming interest? Is it seen as an end in itself or a trust from God? Is church or charitable giving a casual matter or do you tithe (give 10 percent or more)? What are your spending priorities? Are your financial goals different from mine? Do you hold money tightly as a hedge against future economic storms or do you think money is for enjoyment now?

"Money is the root of all evil," goes the common misquotation of the Bible. But this leaves out the real culprit, human nature. Money is neutral, but people can become passionate about it. The apostle Paul actually wrote, "The *love* of money is a root of all kinds of evil" (1 Timothy 6:10, italics mine). Money-love has wrecked not only first marriages, but also remarriages, even those of supposedly "older and wiser" people.

A BIBLICAL PERSPECTIVE ON WHAT WE OWN AND ARE

For a Christian, a biblical perspective on life is important, and it begins with God. Though we talk about what *we* earn or what *we* own, in reality everything belongs to God and comes from his hand. Paul asked, "What do you have that you did not receive? And if you did receive it, why do you boast as though you did not?" (1 Corinthians 4:7). This principle is also true about our own lives: "You are not your own; you were bought at a price" (1 Corinthians 6:19–20).

From such passages as Genesis 1:27–29, it's clear that God has placed the management responsibility for his earth squarely on us. The psalmist said, "You made him [humanity] ruler over the works of your hands; . . . all flocks and herds, . . . birds of the air, . . . fish of the sea" (Psalm 8:6–8).

Whether illustrations of this management principle use the word servant, slave, steward, or manager, the Bible portrays us as caretakers, not owners. In Greek imagery the word for steward referred to a household manager. The classic example of this in ancient times was Joseph in Egypt, managing everything for Pharaoh, including land, crops, and people. None of that wealth belonged to Joseph; he only managed it. That's also true of our lives—we are only managers.

Jesus spoke of both a good manager and a wicked one in his teaching in Matthew 24:45–51. While we choose what type of manager we will be, Jesus showed that all of us will be held accountable to God.

There are many ways by which we demonstrate the kind of steward or manager we are. One is our handling of income. In Malachi 3:8, the people asked God, "How do we rob you?" He answered, "In tithes and offerings." The people were supposed to bring more than a tenth of their harvest or wealth to the temple, but they had not. Because they didn't recognize God as the source of their possessions, they ignored their responsibility to him. What people do with their money in any century is a telling indicator of their character.

In the parable of the shrewd manager (Luke 16), Jesus proclaimed, "No servant can serve two masters. Either he will hate the one and love the other, or he will be devoted to the one and despise the other. You cannot serve both God and Money" (verse 13). Make sure that your prospective partner's attachment to money is not so strong that the two of you will not be able to spend, save, invest, and give money away without constant conflict.

A particular problem arises when one person has consistently tithed, but their prospective spouse has not. This situation often brings contention, unhappiness, and compromised convictions.

Besides being accountable for money, we are also responsible for our use of time, abilities, energy, influence, thoughts, our bodies, the world of nature, and the Gospel itself—all gifts from God. The question is, how does the potential partner treat these? Are they viewed as an offering to God? Every couple has the right and responsibility to reach agreement on these issues before the wedding.

The final test of a manager is faithfulness. "Now it is required that those who have been given a trust prove faithful" (1 Corinthians 4:2). Anyone considering remarriage should be familiar with the prospective spouse's track record. Has he or she been faithful?

LIFESTYLE IN REMARRIAGE

Those who casually view the remarriage scene may think that many of the marriages are designed to improve the partners' financial position. For some this may be so, but only 30 percent of the people I surveyed acknowledged so much as a minor financial reason to marry. In any senior remarriage, combined incomes generally result in greater security and may also improve the quality of life. But a financial bail-out is not high on the list of concerns. When money is the objective, then a con game is probably being played out. The money issue more frequently shows itself in other ways.

For instance, what will it mean if there is full integrity of character in each party, yet great financial inequity between the two? If the woman has accumulated enough wealth to be financially independent but the man has not, how will this affect the man's self-esteem? If the roles are reversed and their past lifestyles have been quite different, how will that work out?

This was what Lance and Rana faced. Rana was a self-employed businesswoman, so she didn't have to marry for financial reasons. Yet as Lance put it, "She was very conscious of the fact that the public perceives me as wealthy because of where I live and where I am in this stage of my business life."

Rana now accompanies Lance on his major business and recreational trips across the world with ease. From all appearances the two seem to have become one. But situations such as this may require capable premarital counseling.

Whether remarried widowed persons have brought great wealth into a new marriage or practically none, the questions of who will handle current income and expenditure will have to be faced. Each spouse has had a period of independent financial decision making. Neither one may surrender that independence easily, and one partner may see the role of money manager as a means of controlling the marriage.

Sometimes, both partners in the new marriage were the guardians of the treasury in their previous marriages. How do they avoid a power struggle? An agreement prior to the wedding can lessen or eliminate tension as the new marriage begins.

HOW MUCH INCOME WILL WE HAVE?

For the more wealthy this question may be one of only limited interest. However, for most remarrieds, that question affects both daily living and financial security in the future. As with fixed assets, one of the surest ways to undermine the new marriage is for one spouse to try to hide part of their income from the other. The commitment to fully disclose finances must be in place before the marriage vows are made.

For the older widowed person, surprise is not a happy word when questions about Social Security and pension rights have not been fully discussed in advance. Social Security benefits are the only income for 14 percent of all seniors receiving such benefits. They are also 90 percent of the income for 24 percent of these seniors.[1]

Could the widow be the loser in a new marriage? Until 1978, a widow of any age lost her income from Social Security by remarrying, forcing many older couples to live together. In 1978, the law was changed. Data from the National Center for Health Statistics show that the number of remarriages for men sixty-five and older jumped 20 percent in 1979. The increase was 36 percent for women.[2] For a sizeable number of couples, Social Security regulations did influence whether they formalized their relationship or not.

However, a surprise could await a couple today if they are not aware that benefits might still be lost. According to a Social Security document, "Benefits continue if a widow, widower, or surviving divorced spouse sixty or older marries."[3] Note the age cut-off.

This was not a surprise for Esther and Loren. They faced the loss of her Social Security if they did not wait another eighteen months to marry. Esther said, "We figured we didn't need it and hopefully won't in the future. We decided that at our age it was more important to be together."

For others to be sure about their specific circumstances, they should consult their local Social Security office and obtain a printed statement of the current policy.

It is also wise to check if remarriage will affect a company pension a widow has been receiving. Laws and regulations are frequently changing the rules in favor of the beneficiary, but nothing should be taken for granted. One widow discovered that while the pension continued after remarriage, the medical coverage connected with it did not. While discovering a negative effect on the couple's future income from any source may not change the decision to marry, learning of it after the marriage could strain the relationship.

HOW WILL INCOME AND EXPENSE BE HANDLED?

Lance and Rana were both in business before they got married. Rana explained their monthly cashflow this way: "He earns the money and I pay the bills. He does not write checks on our personal account. I have my business account. I can make purchases out of our joint account or my business account. Out of our separate business accounts I take care of all my business expense and Lance takes care of all the expense on the properties he owns. We share in the gift giving."

That gift giving is no minor item. Lance and Rana love to share generously with the children and grandchildren from both sides of their marriage. They are also involved in a variety of church and charitable projects.

Some do everything fifty-fifty. When I asked another couple how they handled their current finances, the husband began with this explanation: "On expenses, like the rent, we go fifty-fifty, as well as on the phone and the food bills. There isn't anything we do that we don't go fifty-fifty on. I know that in a lot of marriages money matters can cause problems. But we decided before we got married how we would do it, and that's what we're doing."

I wondered why they didn't put their income together at the beginning of the month. The wife responded first: "He keeps his income and I keep mine and we divide the bills. He pays some and I pay some." Then the husband added: "I guess it never entered our mind to put current income together. It just seemed we fit into this pattern."

Loren and Esther were more detailed in their comments.

Loren began: "I give her a monthly check to carry at least my share of the expenses here at home. We use two different banks because we don't want the bank to mix up our accounts. We both have considerable business yet that we are involved in, and a mix-up could happen since we have the same name. So we keep our affairs separate.

"When we go out or on long trips we share equally in the expense. This is what we wanted to do, this was our agreement. Since we both have about the same amount of money, why shouldn't we share?"

Esther added: "But for monthly bills he gives me a check and I pay all of them. If we go out and buy plants for the yard, we share that and a lot of other things. Like when we bought the furniture, he bought some and I bought some."

Loren: "And like the car. . . . She paid $5,000 and I paid $5,000."

Esther: "And we pay all our income taxes separately."

Loren: "We're afraid that if we get involved in filing together, it could get things confused. We don't have the same amount coming in every month. Some comes in twice a year. And I have a trust. There are a lot of little things like that. It isn't that we don't trust each other. I trust her completely. It's a matter of this works best for us."

Some pool everything. In contrast with those who split all expenses, other couples in the interviews spoke just as strongly and in detail about pooling all current income. Erin and Edna said: "That's the way we feel it should be. At least for us. Our income is about equal. So we combine our incomes."

Ed described his and Tammy's arrangement: "We put all our income in one basket and both of us carry the basket. For our regular income we closed our old accounts and opened a new one. Each of us has a checkbook on it."

Angie outlined the plan she and Eric use: "We merge our incomes. We have one bank account. I had heard before we married how some people fight over money so I said to him, 'I want an understanding now. I don't want you to ever complain about anything I buy. I'm conservative, but I don't always buy things that I desperately need.' We are both very conservative people but if we want to buy something, we do it. But I wasn't sure of myself at the time. Many times a wife has to account for every penny to her husband, even if she's working and putting money in the bank.

"In our case, since he was a tax accountant, he handles the budget. I take care of the bills but he is the one who balances things up. We don't actually live by a budget but we do have to plan for things like trips and not take off whenever we want."

Norene explained how she and David handled their money: "Whatever works well is fine. If David felt like he wanted to handle the budget, that would be good. But he prefers not to and I do it well. So . . .

> I *pay the bills.*
> We *discuss major purchases,*
> *Pool our income,*
> *Tithe on the total,*
> *Save quite a bit each month, and*
> *Live on the rest.*

Her poetic summary of their plan sets forth a workable, trusting arrangement that reflects their faith and commitment.

The returns on the written questionnaire confirmed this variety in handling monthly household finances. Over two-thirds of the people in the survey combine all their income, regardless of amount, and then pay their bills with that family money. One out of six respondents said each spouse paid certain bills from their own income. One out of ten, instead of combining, puts an agreed amount in a common fund for bills and then each controls his or her own income. The remainder use other systems.

PROTECTING THOSE DOLLARS

But what if a major health disability should threaten either the income or fixed assets? Because one spouse is considered financially responsible for the other, the cost of health care and its impact on the budget needs to be recognized. Are both the husband and wife covered by group health insurance? If not, how will health costs be met? Will an individual health policy need to be purchased? Each decade that goes by in a person's life increases the possibility of more severe and long-lasting health problems.

If the couple is retired and on Medicare, does each have a Medigap policy to cover the costs Medicare does not? If not, is monthly income sufficient to cover a major illness or accident? Medigap policies that will cover everything but prescription drugs are available at affordable rates for many retirees. Some policies even cover prescriptions.

More significant are the nightmare costs of long-term nursing home care. Stroke, cancer, and Alzheimer's disease are the more common problems which often require facilities and assistance that home care cannot provide. Under the most recent provision of Medicare, only skilled nursing home needs are covered. Most people require only intermediate or custodial care which still costs about the same. These costs can quickly devour regular income and all other resources.

Medicaid will also pay for skilled nursing home costs but not for intermediate or custodial care. Until recently, a person had to use up all his financial resources before qualifying for Medicaid. This often left the healthy mate impoverished. Under the new law, married persons can protect half of their total assets, up to $60,000, and still qualify for Medicaid. But the assets surrendered to pay the medical costs could be assets accumulated by the healthy spouse before the remarriage. This situation is particularly likely if the ill spouse brought few financial resources to the new marriage.

An increasing number of insurance companies are offering long-term health care policies. Varying amounts of coverage can be purchased and this can help pay for as many as three or four years of care. These policies cover not only skilled nursing home care, but also intermediate and custodial care. Unless the policy is purchased when the insured persons are in their fifties or sixties, however, the cost can be prohibitive.

The principle options for financing health costs are to pay for them yourself, purchase insurance coverage, rely on government programs, or a combination of those three options. The price tag can be high.

These few paragraphs can in no way answer all questions or provide all the information needed, but they can alert couples about possible pressures on their income. There is no substitute for a consultation with Social Security (Medicare) or Medicaid offices, your insurance agent, and groups such as the American Association of Retired Persons. Planning ahead can help to avoid financial disasters from unexpected health problems, and also reduce the tension created when problems appear.

TO HANDLE MONTHLY INCOME:

1. Get agreement on the details. The discussion needs to take place and the agreement be reached before the wedding ceremony.
2. Both parties must be satisfied that this is the best choice for them in their particular circumstance. A borrowed lifestyle that is rigidly imposed will not work.
3. For the couple with a biblical commitment, mutually agreed on theological and practical principles need to be used in the management of money and other assets.
4. Just as it is wise to protect assets (as explained in chapter 5), consideration needs to be given to protect-

ing other resources including income. Never underestimate the consequences of a catastrophic accident or illness.

RESOURCES

American Association of Retired Persons (AARP). Membership is for those over age fifty. Many publications are available (some free to members, others at nominal prices) on a wide variety of subjects of interest to the older American. Excellent research center. National Headquarters: 1909 K. Street. N.W., Washington, D.C., 20049, Phone 202-872-4700 for referral to appropriate department.

Social Security Administration. All information including requests for pamphlets has been centralized at 1-800-234-5772. There are local offices in major cities but phone numbers have not been listed in recent years. Office locations can be found either in the white pages of the phone book under Social Security or in a special section in most cities on colored paper in the front of the directory. Look under Federal Offices, U.S. Government, Health and Human Services.

Medicare. Since it is related to the Social Security Administration, use the number given above. Your operator will make any referrals for further information.

Medicaid. This program is administered by the states, not the federal government. It functions under different names in the various states. It focuses on medical care for those with low incomes or those who have exhausted their resources through long-term illness. Check both the white pages and any special section in the front of the phone directory where city, county, state and federal offices are listed. One state official suggested the networking approach; call a state number (such as the Department of Human Resources) and keep asking for referrals until you locate the proper office in your state.

Medigap. This term is applied to any private insurance policy that covers medical costs that Medicare does not. Call your insurance agent or AARP. Only one good policy is necessary. Use these resources also for special long-term policies that cover nursing home costs.

Insurance. To check on insurance company ratings or to answer any questions you have about a company, look in your phone directory listing for State Offices, Insurance Division.

7

In Sickness and in Health

One of the things that moved me deeply as I interviewed most of these couples was the courageous fulfillment of their wedding vows. The traditional ". . . for better, for worse . . . in sickness and in health . . ." was taken seriously. Whether it was a thirty-three-year-old professional who put his life on hold for three years to give personal care to his dying wife, or a senior who had nursed two mates through final illnesses, all demonstrated that they knew the meaning of commitment.

Nevertheless when it comes time to remarry, the health of a potential partner is an important question to answer. The possibility of losing another mate generally lurks in the back of any widowed person's mind when considering remarriage.

According to the *World Almanac*, in 1988 the life expectancy was 71.5 years for men and 78.3 for women. The March 1989 Demographic Supplement of the U.S. Census Bureau shows that there were 11.6 million widows, but only 2.3 million widowers in the nation. Statistically, the chance of a repeat loss is greater for women. But both parties need to evaluate their ability to handle a second or even third loss. They also need to be open with each other about their own health.

Even a loss at a young age makes the widowed more aware of the brevity of life and more concerned about the future. Kent, the young professional who was widowed at thirty-three, remarried at age thirty-five. While he did not hesitate to marry again, he knows firsthand that there is no immunity from death. He has been comfortable in talking about the subject with his wife Donna. "I have even told her I want her to remarry if something should happen to me," he said. Most of the younger widowed persons I interviewed did not seem as significantly concerned with questions of health.

OLDER PEOPLE'S HEALTH

There is much misinformation about the health of older people. "National studies indicate that 20 percent of all people over the age of 65 will use a nursing home at some point in their lives," stated an article in *Pacific Northwest* magazine. "The longer you live, however, the greater the chance you'll require nursing home care. Nursing home use increases dramatically with age. One out of every 100 persons in the 65 to 74 age group is in a nursing home on a given day. This number increases to 7 out of 100 in the 75 to

84 age group, and to more than 1 out of 5 in the 85 and older group."[1]

When looked at dispassionately, those figures need not be frightening. It would be like heaven, literally, if no one had to use nursing home care. But let's look at these statistics a different way. Ninety-nine percent of people age sixty-five to seventy-four are *not* using nursing home facilities on a given day. Eighty-three percent in the next age group are not. And about 80 percent are not using a nursing home at any given time, even after age eighty-five.

The use of a nursing home by an older person is not necessarily the end of the line. The Oregonian reported, "The number of nursing home residents discharged alive is more than double the number who die in homes."[2]

Independent living, assisted care at home, or assisted care in a retirement center are all options that are used instead of nursing homes by 80 percent of those over age sixty-five.

We should also consider the general level of seniors' activity. The number of well-known and not-so-well known productive older citizens is legion. Famous contemporary seniors include President Reagan who was still in office at age seventy-eight, Representative Claude Pepper who died in office at age eighty-eight, and entertainer George Burns, still active in his nineties. On the church scene, Billy Graham, who is now past seventy, keeps a busy schedule ministering world-wide. Most of us today are personally acquainted with many people in their eighties and beyond who lead active, even vigorous lives. While in her nineties, a woman friend of mine rode a camel when she visited the Pyramids.

One researcher found that "Even people with many

physical ailments rated their health as good—perhaps recognizing that at their age one has to expect some little aches and pains. . . . Men have a greater tendency to deny poor health. High morale for men depends on a self-concept of good health."[3]

COULD I HANDLE LOSING ANOTHER MATE?

Most couples interviewed talked readily about the subject of health and their concerns before remarrying. Isabel, who wanted a man with teeth, hair, and no protruding stomach, told me her feelings about remarriage when she was widowed the first time: "I thought a lot about marrying again. If we got married and one of us had a stroke the day after, did I love him enough to be willing to marry him? I decided I did and we married. I had to take care of him the last two years [of a seventeen-year marriage]."

Isabel recognized that only genuine, deep love could carry her through a second time of extended care for another partner. She made her decision with her eyes open.

Nancy described the time she and Ken (twice widowed) discussed their future while they were dating: "We were very honest. I'll never forget the day. We were traveling down to the beach . . . and got to talking about health. I told him frankly that I had a cancer threat thirteen years ago. But I had been going back to the doctor every three months to get my blood tested and everything has been negative for eleven years. So then Ken said that he had a cancer threat too several years ago. Mine was a chronic lymphocytic leukemia, a very slow-moving disease. The doctor told me some people live thirty years with it. So it was not what would be called an immediate threat.

"I think it's very important to talk about it. Also I made it plain that if he had a long illness, I would not object to caring for him or being responsible. But I said to him, 'How could you face that after losing two wives? Better think about it, because who knows what this could come to.' We both agreed that each of us would gladly face whatever came. We felt that the Lord would provide the grace. We didn't have any fears."

PROCESS DEATH AND SUDDEN DEATH

Twice-widowed Emily, who lost her second husband from a heart attack, said, "I don't think I would have taken on someone who was bedridden right at first. . . . The first time I was widowed I had gone through a long period, six years, when he was very ill. But when you love someone that much you want to help him. So it didn't seem like I was giving too much. It was what I wanted to give." Then almost as a wistful afterthought, remembering those intense years, she added, "But I wouldn't want to take it on again right away."

Emily's reflective comments beautifully illustrate the sensitive yet conflicting human emotions often at work in the lives of those considering remarriage. This is more typical of those who have gone through a process-death rather than a sudden loss.

In process-death, the anxiety is in remembering the physical and emotional exhaustion which months or years of caring bring. When a mate is lost suddenly, the loss itself predominates. With process-death, the primary question often is "Do I have the energy and will to do that again if it becomes necessary?" With sudden death, the important question is often, "Could I handle the shock of losing another mate that way?"

Eric, an accountant, methodically thought through the health question before marrying Angie. "I think we discussed that quite a bit," he recalled. "Because my [first] wife had been ill a long time, I was apprehensive about having the same thing again. And I think Angie was concerned the same way. . . . I got a physical exam and showed her the report. Health was a pretty important factor to us." Certainly there could be no greater openness than Eric showed, unless a prospective mate had an interview with the physician along with the patient.

EMOTIONAL SECURITY

Sometimes a spouse's emotional well-being needs to be discussed along with the issue of physical health. Emotional health is linked to physical well-being and can directly affect the marriage relationship.

Bert cared for his critically ill wife for several years before her death, but unfaithfulness by Elsie's first husband ultimately destroyed her marriage. When Elsie spoke about Bert's health, she said: "I had not gone through illness with my spouse. But I had a complete physical and Bert did too. We were both given a clean bill of health. So we accepted each other as whole persons at that point.

"He has said to me that if ever anything happens to me, he would do it again. And I would be willing to take care of him if necessary. My one request of him was that he not leave me. After being rejected the first time, that has haunted me. He has reassured me again and again. He's been very affirming. I've appreciated that a lot, for it was my biggest hurdle."

COMMITMENT

Bert recalled the final critical years with his first wife and how they related to his new wife, Elsie: "I felt like I had kept my commitment, not out of dogged determination, but out of total life commitment. That was the only integrity I had to offer this woman [Elsie]. She needed to know that integrity because someone walked out on her."

The key word in Bert's statement is *commitment*. His understanding of its meaning and practice grew out of a higher commitment to God as one who knows Jesus Christ as Savior and Guide for life.

Yet Bert knew also that the Christian life is not easy; painful losses come. The six years of faithful service to his cancer-stricken wife brought depth to Bert's understanding of commitment. The psalmist described it when he asked, "Lord, who may dwell in your sanctuary?" That is, who can experience God's close presence? The one "who keeps his oath even when it hurts" (Psalm 15:1, 4).

Commitment is hanging in there no matter how tough it gets. But it's more than that. Real commitment is rooted in the great Commitment Keeper himself who promised, "Never will I leave you; never will I forsake you" (Hebrews 13:5).

FACING AND ACCEPTING RISKS

"David is twelve years older than I am," Norene explained. "Suddenly married to a man this much older than myself has plunged me into the older generation. I became the grandmother of fifteen and great-grandmother of one. All at once our friends are older than I. And I've been forced to think about retirement, that it's just around the corner. He is getting to the age when people start dying. I have spent some time worrying about losing him."

Norene's frank words contrast with the comment of many older people I have heard say, "if something should happen to me. . . ." Those words are a euphemism. Reality demands the recognition that something *will* happen to them and to every one of us. That something is death.

The important thing is to face the subject of illness and death openly and to plan realistically, realizing that one partner in a remarriage will most likely be widowed again. Many of those interviewed had talked freely with each other about death, and their experience had increased their ability to deal with another loss.

I saw courage and compassion merged in the lives of Erin and Edna. Both of them were completely open about their health. Erin couldn't avoid it. Parkinson's disease was sending its signals while they courted. Both are now seventy-two years old. The Parkinson's makes Erin self-conscious. He says some days he is shakier than others. Edna simply says, "All people have one disability or another. We go shopping together and to plays. He still drives."

Before their marriage Erin was concerned about Edna's knowledge of Parkinson's and her willingness to see him through it. He had misgivings about getting married and making himself a burden. He said he had "spent a fortune on his second wife's illness."

"The disease does not bother me," said Edna. "Many people say he is much better since he remarried—mentally, emotionally and physically. We enjoy being with each other and that's what we wanted."

Willard Kohn, who with his second wife, Jane, wrote of his life as a widower, gave a good summary about risk-taking: "Any venture one undertakes involves risk, and so it is with remarriage. A young man may remarry and find that his wife cannot love his young children; this can be heartbreaking. A middle-aged man may remarry and falter under the burden of playing middle-man between his wife and his children.

"An elderly gentleman or lady may be more subject to illnesses and to an early death. Yet . . . the joy and blessing they have from being together in their later years far outweigh the risk of sadness and tears which will surely come to one or the other."[4]

LEGAL DOCUMENTS AND HEALTH

Just as there are legal steps an individual or a couple may want to take regarding finances as they begin a new marriage, there is also an opportunity to consider options related to health.

Many people are deeply disturbed by the rapid advance of medical technology that can keep a body alive almost indefinitely. Physicians struggle to maintain a balance between their training to prolong life and their understanding that death must come to us all. Many of us expect health workers to make heroic efforts to sustain physical life. Yet people are revolted by the stories they hear of bodies without inner life being kept physically alive in hospitals for months and years. Many people are saying, "That's not for me."

The *Living Will* is intended to express a person's desires regarding the use of heroic efforts and life support systems. It gives directions to family members and medical professionals in situations, such as being in a coma, where the person cannot communicate. In states where such a living will is legal, you can get a copy to examine either from your doctor or your state health department.

Earlier, we discussed the legal tool known as power of attorney. This document can also be used to allow a specified person to express your will for you regarding final decisions on life support systems and heroic resuscitation efforts. In cooperation with the American Association of Retired Persons, the American Bar Association distributes a booklet on this subject, *Health Care Powers of Attorney.*[5]

Any decisions you make about living wills or power of attorney will need to be made with the full knowledge and understanding of your spouse. Then, if the need arises, your spouse will know what legal documents are available to help them deal with the situation.

Health, sickness, and death are subjects some people want to deny or postpone discussing. But by talking about them now and arriving at satisfying decisions, a couple provides important peace of mind for each other in the future.

THREE THINGS TO REMEMBER:

1. The general health of seniors is far better than most people think.

2. Full disclosure of health conditions to each partner before remarriage helps build trust and prepares for a more willing, loving response in the face of illness and disabilities.

3. People who have gone through months or years of caring for a terminally ill spouse demonstrate a high degree of commitment and compassion. This proven inner strength enables them to remarry even while recognizing the risk. It also helps potential new mates to have confidence in marrying them.

8

Speaking of Sex ...

During the week of Valentine's Day a couple years ago, CBS *This Morning* propelled viewers through scenes of older persons finding companions via video dating services or computer-generated electronic mail. On one program, Harry Smith discussed love and marriage with guests who were seniors. During the lively interaction, one man commented, "I blew my stack when I found out my son was living in a co-ed dorm in the 1960s."

Twenty-five years later, the same father is retired and widowed. Now he himself is living with a woman. His explanation for his new attitude is simple: The nation's values have changed.

More and more seniors are living together with no plans to marry, reported Harry Smith. In fact, he alleged, the greatest increase in co-habitation within any age group is among seniors. While only three out of ten Americans approve of unmarried couples living together, little restraint is put on seniors, according to Smith. Whatever the reliability of these figures, just hearing them on a CBS news program gives them credibility for many people.

Other researchers verify this pattern among seniors. Bernard Starr and Marcella Weiner in *Sex and Sexuality in the Mature Years*, say that "For a majority, living together without marriage is acceptable."[1]

More startling was the response to one of their research questions: "How do you feel about older men and women without partners going to prostitutes to relieve sexual needs?" Many were for it; 64 percent of the women and 74 percent of the men approved.[2]

Speaking of pre-marital sex among the general public, Christian counselor and author Jim Talley confirms that, "according to recent secular research, the percentage among formerly married persons is as high as ninety-five percent."[3]

Dr. John White, associate professor of psychiatry at the University of Manitoba, makes a keen observation on "normal" sexual activity: "All science can say is that it is 'a statistical norm,' that is, that the majority of people do it. *Normal* and *average* do not mean the same thing, however. When a Christian talks about something being normal, he is talking about it being 'as it was meant to be.' The scientist, on the other hand, knows nothing of meaning or purpose. He can only describe what he sees. And to him the normal means 'the way things are,' not the way they should be."[4]

The statistics above tell us little restraint is practiced in the population at large and that the majority of people opt for sexual activity outside of marriage, although this trend may have been slowed by the AIDS scare. But the widowed have a choice. Commitment to a biblical perspective not only calls for abstinence, but it also enables people to be obedient to that call.

The man's excuse on CBS that "the nation's values have changed" can satisfy him because his life-roots are in the shallow soil of pop-culture. He shares in social values made barren by a lack of biblical teaching in recent generations. The Bible, however, calls for abstinence outside of marriage.

SOME BIBLICAL LIGHT

I asked one young, remarried widow to rate the needs that moved her toward marriage on a scale from "none" to "very much." At the word *sexual*, her voice brightened and she said, "Oh, yes, very much!" This legitimate drive will vary from person to person, but no one can ignore it.

It is not enough to tell the suddenly single, "Just say no" or "Take the cold shower cure." Many in society will criticize determined celibates for having emotional or sexual hang-ups. They may try to convince them that sex outside of marriage is normal.

The apostle Paul recognized human passion: "Now to the unmarried and the widows I say: It is good for them to stay unmarried, as I am. But if they cannot control themselves, they should marry, for it is better to marry than to burn with passion" (1 Corinthians 7:8–9).

Later, Paul encouraged Christians to beat temptation: "No temptation has seized you except what is common to man. And God is faithful; he will not let you be tempted beyond what you can bear. But when you are tempted, he will

also provide a way out so that you can stand up under it"
(1 Corinthians 10:13).

To know that Jesus was not a sexless, colorless person
who moved unfeelingly among people, but that he was a real,
human person helps put iron in our soul. "We have one
[Jesus] who has been tempted in every way, just as we are—
yet was without sin" (Hebrews 4:15).

Singles struggling with the sex drive need to know they
are not alone, that God understands and is gracious and
compassionate. Christ can be both our standard and enabler.

THE PLACE OF THE BODY

"The body is not meant for sexual immorality, but for the
Lord, and the Lord for the body. By his power God raised the
Lord from the dead, and he will raise us also. Do you not
know that your bodies are members of Christ himself? Shall I
then take the members of Christ and unite them with a
prostitute? Never! Do you not know that he who unites
himself with a prostitute is one with her in body? . . . But he
who unites himself with the Lord is one with him in spirit.
Flee from sexual immorality. . . . Therefore honor God with
your body" (1 Corinthians 6:13–20).

The dignity of the human body is basic to the issue of
abstinence. It is so important, that it will be resurrected.
Therefore what people do with their bodies isn't a matter of
indifference. The word used for sexual immorality in the New
Testament consistently refers to any sexual activity outside
marriage. All of 1 Corinthians 7 concerns marriage and sex. It
merits careful study.

The statistic from the Starr-Weiner report on the acceptability of prostitutes for seniors is just that: a statistic indicating what some people choose. The behavior it reports is totally opposed to biblical standards. The book of Proverbs more than once shouts its warning about extra-marital sex. "For the prostitute reduces you to a loaf of bread, and the adulteress preys on your very life" (6:26).

Sexual intercourse was designed by God not just for procreation but also to release us from isolation (Genesis 2:18, 24) and to provide pleasure within the bounds set. When sex is practiced outside marriage, it sets us up for failure in marriage. If we have not been able to maintain abstinence during singleness, how will we maintain it during a mate's long illness or at other times of difficulty in marriage? If illicitness and promiscuity has a hold on us, sex in marriage may quickly turn to boredom.

One couple, typical of those I interviewed, voiced a strong conviction against sexual activity outside marriage. When I asked how they acted during the courting relationship and if they spent time at each other's homes, the man responded: "I spent considerable time at her house and she visited me at my house during the week and after church on Sunday."

His wife added, "For people who are in their fifties and have been married, there is a lot of temptation. As far as sex goes, if it hadn't been for the Lord, there would have been."

When I asked how the sexual pressure compared to that prior to a first marriage, the husband replied: "The pressure may be equal to but not greater than before a first marriage, but the pressure is there."

Both men and women, young and old, have similar feelings and choices. Those who choose to refrain from sex outside of marriage on a biblical basis say they have tried to follow the counsel that "Marriage should be honored by all, and the marriage bed kept pure, for God will judge the adulterer and all the sexually immoral" (Hebrews 13:4).

SOCIETY'S VIEW OF SENIORS AND SEX

How society views seniors and sex has an affect on how they see themselves. Three words, *slow, senile,* and *sexless,* describe seniors for people who cling to stereotypes. One author discussed three repeated themes in sexual myths about seniors: that they are not sexually desirable, sexually desirous, or sexually capable.[5] That author also coined the word *neuterdom* which, she says, is often assigned to anyone over age fifty.

With such attitudes, many seniors tend to gradually assume the role society expects. They accept the myths about themselves. This helps us understand the titters and giggles on so many television comedy shows when sex and seniors are linked. It explains the puzzlement among many adult children of widowed seniors when the possibility of remarriage appears.

It shows why an older man who expresses the least interest in sex becomes a dirty old man to some. Or an older woman becomes a hag or a biddy because she is perceived as having lost her sexiness. We are still in a culture excessively oriented to youth, deluded into thinking sex and sexuality always fade away after fifty. Too many of the elderly have worn actors' garments for a mythical role others have created.

Beauty needs to be redefined to include character,

intelligence, expressiveness, knowledge, achievement, disposition, tone of voice and speech patterns, posture and bearing, warmth, style, and social skills, all of which can be found at any age.[6]

A husband and wife who team-teach a course in human sexuality at Loyola Marymount University in Los Angeles, sum up society's view this way: "Whatever the label, the message is plain. The old are sexually incompetent; their intimacies are a poor imitation of life, their antics being either cutely comic or offensively perverse. Society takes for granted sexual impotence in the elderly."[7]

Part of the explanation for such negative attitudes toward sex in later life comes from our fear of growing old. Better to joke about its supposed downside. This develops into a prejudice called *ageism*. Sometimes subtle, sometimes obvious discrimination is shown toward people simply because they are old.

One thing often overlooked is that sex and sexuality are not the same. In the public mind *sex* or *to have sex* generally refers to intercourse itself. Sex, however, is only that which identifies the human being as male or female at birth. Sexuality is the expression of the whole person emotionally, mentally, and physically. And for the Christian, the spiritual is a vital component influencing and binding the whole being together. The maturing of our sexuality is meant to continue through all of life since change is always taking place.

When human sexuality is seen as a God-given gift, we can allow love and romance to be part of life from age nineteen to ninety. In marriage, love and romance can be tender and sensitive, intimate and sensual at any age. There may be a lot of physical action, including intercourse, or there may be very little if advanced age or health problems interfere. In either case, the gift is still to be enjoyed.

When seniors rebel against the labels of slow, senile and sexless, and while couples quietly proceed with their new romances and marriages, there is hope that the stereotypes will fade.

THE REMARRIEDS SPEAK

For the most part, those interviewed were quite open in telling how they discussed the subject of sexual relations with their prospective mates. And they made comments on the results after marriage. This took courage for many of the oldest ones who would not normally discuss the subject with others. All spoke with little prompting and few questions.

A standard question I posed to each couple was, "In counseling times or apart from them, did you talk about your sexual expectations?"

Lance and Rana, in their early fifties, agreed they did. Then Rana spoke up: "I said when I went out with people that I was going to tell them what they were getting—what kind of person I am, what I like, and that sort of thing. I didn't have any secrets."

Lance added: "We just talked about all aspects of married life. We talked about our first marriages very openly. Talking about them is probably how we got to talking about our expectations. I'll be very frank to say that I didn't know my sex life could be as enjoyable the second time around."

Indicating that her sexual relations were not satisfactory in her first marriage, Rana said: "I felt that if it wasn't great in my second marriage, I could live that way. Not that it hasn't turned out great. It just wasn't as important as how he related to me and my kids and the family."

Nancy, a perky and very attractive grandmother of seventy-nine, spoke freely: "We had absolutely no sexual problems. We enjoy the God-given intimacies that come naturally. And there was no idea that we had to perform like we did when we were first married. We understood that. We were not expecting too much or too little. . . . I never once thought about comparing anything with former days. . . . I think the greatest part of marriage at our age is the intimacy. We're one. And there's no embarrassment. It's just beautiful."

I questioned Erin and Edna. He took the lead: "She probably doesn't want to talk about it, but it's great." Surprisingly, Edna did want to talk about it. "It is. It's marvelous. . . . I wonder if it's attributable to the fact that we don't have any worries. We're comfortable."

In conversation with Eric and Angie they indicated openness with each other both before and after the marriage. Then Angie added: "There was a question at our age [sixty-nine], however, and I made the remark to him, 'You know that [sexual activity] is not the most important part of this marriage. In a younger marriage, maybe it was.'

"And yet people think that older folk are not made the same as younger persons. But you are! You still are! There are times when different medications are taken and people don't function like they should. But we agreed that sex should not be the most important part of marriage. If it should not be as satisfying as expected, then we would find our relationship close in every other way. We never thought sex would interfere, and it has been beautiful."

Not everyone I interviewed had discussed sex with their intended mates before marriage. Norman and Nan said they did not discuss their sexual needs or ask questions before the wedding, except for agreeing that they would have sex. Norman was concerned whether he could perform after being rejected and abandoned by his first wife.

"I told him not to worry about it," Nan said. "Sex is important but there are a lot of other things that are just as important." When a mate can be as reassuring as that, the probability of success is greatly increased.

Two or three couples did not discuss sexual issues at all. They reflected the attitudes of the past when the subject wasn't even discussed between mates, or they believed "doing what comes naturally" took care of it all.

Writers Butler and Lewis may have had such couples in mind when they offered this good advice on communicating with your partner about sex: "Have you ever freely talked to your partner about sex? About what stimulates you the most? Do you feel embarrassed or too awkward to ask? Has your partner ever candidly asked you? Many couples assume that one doesn't have to talk, since sex 'comes naturally.' This is not so. We are all different from one another and we need to express our likes and dislikes rather than merely hope our partners can read our minds or know intuitively how to please us."[8]

Words flowed easily in my interview with David and Norene. "We did discuss the subject," David said. "From my perspective it certainly was an open discussion. My first wife and I did not talk about sex at all. We weren't very open that way. So this was quite new to me. It wasn't hard, just strange. I don't see that there is a great deal of difference between our expectations and what we shared afterward. Part of my openness was due to the teaching at marriage retreats I went on. We had never had an opportunity to learn or discuss such things in the previous church I attended."

Norene jumped into the discussion to say, "After the demise of my short marriage, I went through months of self-doubt about my worth as a person and my worth as a sexual being. I thought I was the failure . . . because this man would not talk about his reasons. He would not go to counseling. . . . He wanted out. I'm the kind that takes on the blame. I felt that I must have done this or that, or been inadequate, or I just couldn't please him. I went to a counselor for several months which helped me lay some of those fears to rest."

David and Norene in their courting practiced what most counselors recommend. They talked with each other about their sexual concerns and willingly attended the classes and counseling provided by their church. Thus they were better prepared to build a satisfying and solid marriage.

Marriage counselors warn about sexual problems that may exist in a remarriage. One church counselor I interviewed gave me this list:

1. A know-it-all attitude based on previous experience.
2. False assumptions about the opposite sex based on the former mate.
3. Reluctance to communicate explicitly for fear of rejection. (Not verbalizing preferences.)
4. Old flashbacks appearing during intimacy, creating response problems.
5. Difficulty in feeling one with the new mate. Some-

times emotional healing and unresolved guilt need professional help.

6. Privacy problems if there are children.

Other problems can develop, such as age differences or health conditions that affect sexual preferences or abilities. A sense of competition with the previous spouse can also affect the sex life. If the marriage is to be a happy one, these will need to be dealt with between the partners or with assistance from outside.

Olga and George, the couple referred to in the introduction, came to the end of their short marriage because of an unresolved sexual problem. George had asked Olga to respond to a sexual preference of his that horrified her. Perhaps his first wife had been cooperative and it was all mutually satisfying, but Olga could not respond. Discussion of sexual preferences and expectations before marriage would have either stopped George and Olga from marrying or prepared them for success.

In the early fifties there weren't many helpful books on intimate relations, and few trained counselors dealt with the subject. Today, that is not the case. Adequate help is available, and there is no excuse for ignoring it.

PREMARITAL AND MARITAL JITTERS

It's not just first-timers who can be swamped by anxiety and apprehension about a planned marriage. Those remarrying can have similar feelings, though for different reasons.

Sometimes performance expectations can be lowered

with a gentle, off-hand comment. One woman reminded her future husband that she was "not a teenager anymore."

In one instance, the wife said, "He hasn't been able to have intercourse on account of his heart." When asked how she responded, she replied, "Well, if I didn't love him I wouldn't stay. But I love him!" And it should be added, a heart problem does not necessarily limit sexual activity. Ask your cardiologist.

Fears from the past came back when Norene starting talking with David about marriage: "I had a hysterectomy and my physical makeup was changing. I didn't know how it would be. And I know that I'm not the same as I was ten or twenty years ago. I'm different in my body, but David reassured me that he loves me and that those changes don't make any difference. He has helped me know that our marriage relationship is far more important."

Men also have misgivings about their bodies. Bert wondered first if he would be able to perform sexually: "During the years my wife was ill I had been inactive. Do I want to take the chance of baring my body, much less my soul to anyone? All those thoughts went through my mind. But it didn't take long for them to go away. We found it very easy to communicate at every level . . . including our sexual concerns."

Elsie added, "I think there was a fear of limited expectations when actually there weren't any—just the fear of them." Many counselors would agree that this is often the case.

There are conflicting medical and psychological opinions whether impotence in men is a physical or psychological problem. It may be either, depending on the person and the circumstances, and can occur at any age.

For older men the fear is often related to surgery: "Impotence following prostate operations usually is psychological rather than physiological in origin. Men do, in fact, sometimes become impotent if they think that impotence is a 'natural' result of the operation; their attitude becomes a self-fulfilling prophecy."[9]

Other upsetting events in life such as marital conflicts, stress, worry, retirement, or bodily changes and disfigurement can all contribute to sexual dysfunction in either men or women.

In case of problems, most counselors suggest seeing a physician first to rule out a medical cause. This is true for many problems, not just sexual ones. However, the physician-author of *Love and Sex After Sixty* says, "Those graduating from medical school before 1961 have had no training in this area [of sexual dysfunctions] . . . most doctors have not had systematic training in the general medical problems of older people."[10]

Agencies such as the National Institute on Aging or the National Institute on Mental Health can supply a list of persons or clinics specializing in geriatrics and gerontology.

Christian author and counselor Willard Harley gives some bittersweet reassurance especially for seniors: "One of the graphic ironies of my job appears when I counsel couples in their seventies for sexual incompatibility. Almost always they resolve their problem within a few weeks, and many experience sexual fulfillment for the first time after forty or fifty years of marriage. 'What a difference this would have made in our marriage,' they often report. While I am happy that they finally resolved a longstanding and frustrating marital problem, I feel sad for the years they unnecessarily endured the guilt, anger, and depression that often accompany sexual incompatibility."[11]

WHAT DO THE EXPERTS SAY?

1. If you are a Christian, review what the Bible has to say about sex and the purpose of the body.
2. Don't let myths stifle your sex life.
3. Adjust your sexual activity to fit your age, health, and mutual preferences.
4. Seek professional help when necessary.
5. Don't forget that touching with love and tenderness goes a long way for either mate.

9
What Will the Children Say?

Let's flip the channel back to NBC's *Empty Nest* and the widowed Dr. Harry Westin. Older daughter Carol, in one of her "down" times is reacting to her father's dating of Eva: "I lost my husband, I lost my mother, and now you!"

Carol's outburst echoes in many homes in similar situations. She is not ready to give up her father to another woman. Carol thinks she will be deprived of her father's emotional support and that Eva is moving in on her mother's territory. In Carol's mind, dad should have been more concerned about her.

As in the Westin household, widowhood, dating, and remarriage may begin or extend a role reversal that often occurs between older parents and their children. When children filch a cookie from the jar or stay out too late, the question in their minds is, "What will Mom and Dad say?"

But when the children are grown, the worried person may now be a widowed parent. If dating or remarriage are possibilities the question becomes, "What will the children say?"

When I surveyed couples about this, 54 percent reported that their adult children encouraged them when they began a new relationship. Forty percent of the children were neutral in their attitude, while 6 percent discouraged it. The fact that the 40 percent withheld their positive encouragement probably indicates they were more negative than either parent or child acknowledged. Whatever their reaction, most children probably have some negative feelings and questions.

I'LL LOSE MY SURVIVING PARENT

Possessiveness, the feeling of ownership, and in some instances the desire to dominate are the unhealthy extremes of love and concern. We see it when a parent cannot release a child from the nest to soar and survive on its own. It is mirrored in an adult child who cannot release his or her widowed parent to take an independent action the child fears. It manifests itself in many forms. One is the fear of losing the remaining parent.

Bert and Elsie had four children each when they remarried; all were living in their own homes except one. In general, all the children affirmed what their parents were doing. When the wedding was certain, Bert sensed that one of Elsie's daughters was concerned that he was taking her mother from her, that once they were married, Elsie wouldn't be available.

"I told her, 'I don't want to take your mom away,' " Bert

recalled. "She said, 'You won't mind if Mom spends time with me?' 'Of course not', I answered. It was one of those 'testing of the waters.'"

When birth parents reassure their children of their continuing love and availability, they help reduce the children's concerns. If the new mate is sensitive, as Bert was, and offers reassurance to the future spouse's children, so much the better. Prevention will avert tension about changing relationships.

The marriage relationship comes first, but concern for the children should not be far behind. This is especially so when adult children feel they are losing their only remaining parent.

There may also be family traditions at stake, such as where to spend Thanksgiving and Christmas. Talk about these emotion-laden times in advance. Adult children may prefer to maintain celebrations in their homes. The remarried, older couple may want their own time together. Families can plan to alternate the location of holiday celebrations. If people don't have to travel far, it's possible to hold an annual reunion for the extended families from both sides.

THE NEW SPOUSE AS INTRUDER

Angie's children were understanding when they first learned of her dating and then her engagement to Eric, except for her daughter, that is.

"My daughter was a Daddy's girl and she felt I pulled that engagement a little too fast," Angie explained. "I had been giving her little signs telling her I'd been seeing this man, that we're good friends and that we did this or that. She'd listen but it wasn't sinking in. To her we would always be just good friends. She loved her Dad so much she couldn't visualize anyone taking his place.

"She said, 'Why didn't you ever bring him around so I could get acquainted with him?' I told her 'Honey, I don't have to have your approval but I've been telling you all the time that this was what I was doing.' It was okay with her to have men as friends but not to have it go any further. Time has healed our relationship."

In another scenario, Della, who is about sixty years old, became angry with her eighty-seven-year-old mother, who was intent on marrying her first husband's business partner. The daughter finally acknowledged her anger and fear saying, "I didn't want Sam taking Pop's place."

We see in both these instances what is often the hardest hurdle to leap: the feeling that a parent's new mate is taking over the deceased parent's place. Once a couple recognizes what is happening, there are steps they can take to resolve the situation.

The potential spouse can put aside personal feelings of rejection and reach out in love and friendship. Depending on the circumstances and ages, it will take personal time with the child or children, or arranging dinner occasions with a married child and spouse. Perhaps a fishing expedition can help a father-son relationship in trouble, or some other appropriate venture if it's for mother and daughter. Somehow, set the scene for spontaneous conversation or even gentle confrontation as necessary.

The widowed parent can also help the children realize that no person can take another's place. No two persons are alike. No child can replace another child. When we adopted an eight-year-old girl eighteen months after the death of our eleven-year-old daughter, Jill did not and could not replace Becky. While there were similarities between the two girls, there were also great differences. The healing for us came not in replacing one girl with another, but in seeing the delightful differences and helping Jill become all she could be.

So it can be when any loved one dies and in due time God provides someone else for us. Children who lose a parent can learn to appreciate another person, not as a replacement, but as a new family member who can help to meet the needs of the surviving parent.

If the child refuses to be reconciled to the situation, time and patience may heal, but some counseling with a pastor or counselor may be needed.

YOU'RE BEING EXPLOITED

Adult children should be concerned about their parent's financial status in a new marriage. Fortune hunters are real predators and the size of the fortune is irrelevant to many. Even people of modest means need to be wary. But children can also overreact.

When Evelyn and Larry were courting they encountered strong resistance from their children. When I asked Evelyn why her son, who lived at a distance, objected to the marriage she said: "He had read a lot of stories and thought I was going to marry someone who would take the home away from me and leave me destitute. He didn't know Larry at all. I tried to tell him that he was someone I had known years ago, but it just went over my son's head."

Then Larry commented, "Her son should have understood that we had known each other for over forty years and I had run around with his Dad. I wouldn't have done anything to hurt his mother."

Evelyn said Larry's two boys were good about the marriage, but his daughter was much the opposite: "She wouldn't acknowledge us at all for a long time and wrote me a real bitter letter. She figured he should remain single the rest of his life, I guess."

While there was no hint from Larry and Evelyn that their children were fearful of losing their inheritance, such fear can be a motive in adult children not wanting their widowed parents to remarry. A legal premarital agreement or a will that covers the issue can defuse those fears. Keepsakes, photos, and special furniture can sometimes be given now rather than at death. A list of those items and their recipients can be added to the will and made known to the family now.

Assurance that these matters are cared for will help avoid hurt feelings now and later. After your death, if certain willed items are unwanted, suggest in advance that the recipient give, trade, or sell undesired items to a family member before disposing of them otherwise.

An accompanying fear of adult children is that if the parent loses his or her financial reserves in a marriage, the children will have to support their parent in a nursing home or other care center. Again, by making every effort to cover such a contingency, the fears will probably fade.

CHILDREN AS CONTROLLERS

While the adult child will probably never use the word *accountability*, that is what some children want from their parent. They perceive their widowed parent as much less competent than when he or she was married. Children need to recognize that the confusion and shock of grief has not made the person permanently incapable of coping.

Author Willard Kohn tells about a friend of his: "Louis, at seventy-seven, found that children inhibited his dating. . . . 'My two daughters were married with families themselves when my wife died, yet they seemed resentful at the thought of their father even thinking about women and dating. They would tell me I was too old or to wait awhile. But at seventy-seven, I didn't have much time. If I was going to spend two or three years looking for a woman, I might as well forget it.'"[1]

This illustrates some of the negative reactions adult children have when a widowed parent is considering remarriage. But children can also choose to be supportive or at least control unwarranted emotional responses.

How can adult offspring know whether they are reacting to reality or to their own fears? After all, they probably have not been in the place where their parent is. They have not faced the loneliness or the emotional, social, mental, and even physical pain caused by loss of a spouse.

An objective counselor may be required. Such a person can help children understand what is going on in a parent who seems to be acting like a teenager. The children may be shocked to discover that the passion they feel is not theirs alone. It is surging in their dating parents. A capable counselor can also calm unnecessary fears or help the children assist their widowed parents if the perceived hazard is real.

CHILDREN AS ENCOURAGERS

Bert and Elsie's two families had been close friends during the children's growing-up years. All were in attendance at the memorial service for Bert's first wife, who had died after a lengthy cancer battle. He tells an interesting story: "After the service, two of our children were talking right there in the building. In the course of the conversation one said to the other, 'When the time is right, I hope our parents will look at each other.' Their encouragement was taking shape within a half hour after the benediction."

One woman told about the reaction of one of her sons. When she called him to say that she was interested in someone, he said "That's great, Mom." The woman added, "When I called later to tell him I had a ring, he whooped over the phone and said 'Right on, Mom!'"

Children can take a great step toward being encouragers when they see their widowed parent as more than a father or mother, more than a grandfather or grandmother. Their parent is an individual determined to pursue God's best and live a full life.

A PARENT'S DECLARATION OF INDEPENDENCE

If the parent-child relationship has matured into adult friendship and mutual respect, it will survive the remarriage of the widowed parent. It may become even stronger.

Whatever happens, the parent needs to make at least three declarations to the child (children):

First, I don't need your "permission" but I would like your

understanding, continuing friendship, and even your encouragement. You and I need each other.

Second, I still love you. I always will, irrespective of my planned (or present) marriage; I will love you despite any rejection or anger on your part.

Third, I do want you to know what I'm doing. Not because I am accountable to you but because I want to build an even greater openness and sharing between us.

A suitor can build bridges to the children of the intended mate by doing what Bert did. He had known Elsie's children many years: "I called her oldest son and told him I had asked his mom out on a date. I asked him if he felt okay about me dating her. I told him I had no intention of running around and playing the field. My intention was to ask his mother to marry me (she knew nothing of this). After some comments he said, 'If you can make my mother happy, go for it!'"

Being thoughtful and considerate of the feelings of your intended mate's children helps to disarm any suspicion and turn negatives into positives. Consultation with the children and bringing them into the plans is wise, but don't let them control; be fair, but firm. And who knows? You might learn something from them that could make this planned marriage unwise. More likely, everyone will be happier and better prepared for the celebration of the "I do's" and the years to come.

REVIEW THE PARENT/ADULT CHILD RELATIONSHIP BY ASKING:

1. Have both of you offered reassurance of your love and continuing concern to your own children and to the children of your future spouse?

2. Will you help your children understand that no one can replace their lost parent, but that another mate will add strength and blessing to their lives if they allow it to happen?

3. Can you be patient when the children overreact in their effort to protect you? Listen. They may see something you don't.

4. Are your children trying to make decisions for you that you feel are not theirs to make? Will you define the parameters of your relationship with them in this new situation so they will realize when they have gone beyond concern to control?

5. Will you make your own declaration of independence constructively so you won't shut the door to your children?

10

What about Young Children?

Darryl and Lisa were both active in their church when they remarried. She had been widowed and he divorced a few years earlier while they were in their mid-thirties. Without their determination to keep this new commitment, Darryl and Lisa's marriage would have been another divorce statistic.

The smiles and laughter we shared as I interviewed them in their home belied the seriousness of Darryl's comment when we talked about the effect of young children on a second marriage: "I've said that if I were to write a book on remarriage, the first chapter would have but one word: DON'T! That's the way I felt after the first three or four years. That is, I'd say it at least while there are children at home. It is so hard ... so much pain ... and scars that last."

Darryl was able to bare his raw feelings because he and

Lisa had won their struggle. It's insights from couples like them that help other people who have children at home and are planning to remarry. It can be tough, but there are rewards.

BIRTH OF A STEPFAMILY

"Every stepfamily is born of loss," John Fisher, a California psychiatrist notes. "Each family member has experienced the tragedy of divorce or death or separation from a parent or spouse; the aftershock can linger on for years."[1]

The younger widowed person may marry someone else who is widowed, never-married, or divorced. At this age there are still many never-married people available, and with the present divorce rate, the supply of divorced persons is ample too. But other widows or widowers are not as available.

When the younger widowed think of remarrying, many of their concerns are the same as those of seniors. However, when minor children are involved, the questions to be asked and the difficulties to be prepared for are quite different. Young children may not be able to verbalize their feelings and concerns, but those emotions are real. They can be even more explosive than adults' feelings and may call for many years of patient work.

Adult children of the widowed make their impact on a remarriage from outside the home. Minor children affect the new husband and wife from within the home with a dailyness that can't be escaped.

BLENDING FAMILIES

The term *blended family* refers to the effort to bring together the children and single parents from two different families to form a new family. Jim Smith of the Family Life Center, Highland Park Presbyterian Church in Dallas, Texas, says that the idea that a stepfamily is the same as a traditional family is a myth: "This establishes unrealistic assumptions for stepfamilies that often create rules and role expectations which are not workable. Stepfamilies are unique and cannot be expected to function like first-marriage families."[2]

Other experts in the field of marriage counseling, as well as the couples themselves, often observe that *The Brady Bunch* is not a realistic picture of life in a blended family.

Because Lisa and Darryl's marriage almost didn't survive, I asked what saved it. Lisa said: "All of us went for family counseling. But we waited almost a year before we went. We had no idea the marriage would be as difficult as it was."

Darryl added, "In retrospect we should have had premarital counseling on blending families. We read some books, had some ideas, and knew some people who had gone through it. But it's like a toothache: You don't know what it's like until you have one."

To minimize the negative impact and to accentuate the positive aspects of a blended family, seek competent professional counseling before remarriage. Go to someone who understands and works regularly with blended families.

BONDING

In many ways Everett and Ingrid echo Darryl and Lisa. Everett was a widower with two young boys under age five, but Ingrid had never been married. During the interview she thrust her needle in and out of her needlepoint pattern. Very much a take-charge person, she jabbed her words home: "We have paid a price ... stress ... hard feelings. I'm trying to learn when to press my points and when to back out. He had been a complacent, detached father in his first marriage. I don't want to whip out my whistle and expect them [the children] to march to the beat. But I want them to learn to be responsible."

Everett said, "One thing I'd like others to know is, 'Don't assume the bonding between the new parent and children is going to happen easily.' I thought the boys would naturally accept Ingrid as their mother. At first it didn't surface much. But over the years it has become obvious that they have not accepted her in her role as mother or authority figure." He and Ingrid are still working their way through blending and bonding.

Family expert Jim Smith said that the idea that love happens instantly is yet another of the myths of the blended family: "Many stepparents feel that they should love and care about their stepchildren as if they were their own. Or they may expect their stepchildren to love them quickly, especially for all the work stepmom has done and all the sacrifices she has made for the children."[3] Such ideas put unrealistic pressure on all concerned.

FAMILY ISSUES

I asked Darryl and Lisa to describe some of the issues they faced: "Was it confrontation between two mates, between one mate and the other's children, or between two sets of children?"

"All of the above!" was Darryl's quick response. And we all laughed.

"Discipline was one thing," Darryl continued. "Her son and mine were very different, though the same age. The boys had a lot of conflict, and Lisa and I had difficulty understanding each other and how we had disciplined our own children."

Lisa: "He'd stand up for his kids and I'd stand up for mine and then the kids would fight all the more."

Darryl: "We had each been raising our own kids—this worked for us and that worked for them. We didn't come together in marriage as young people trying to experience the world. We came as people who had experience and knew what worked for us."

Everett and Ingrid had to face a similar situation. Everett recalled: "The boys are very manipulative. They would pit us against each other. We've had to work very hard to make it a team effort with the boys."

In many families the typical confrontation between a teenager and stepparent ends with the shout, "I don't have to obey you. You're not my real father!" When these things are said in the blended family, it isn't always clear whether it's part of the usual teenage rebellion or deep anger toward the stepparent.

Blending and bonding in the younger remarried family is often more difficult because during the time of singleness a child may become "best friend" to the parent. Girls will often begin to take over the management of the house for their parent. When the remarriage takes place, the child goes back to being a child and loses out to the new mate. Resentment easily bubbles to the surface.

It can also be a shock for a never-married man or woman to marry a previously married person with children. The never-married person suffers an immediate loss of privacy, and this can delay relationship-building for everyone.

Karen, a widow with four children, married Gene, a single man. She said, "Gene has no time or space now, where before all he had was those. It was a tough adjustment for a single man to move into a ready-made home. The kids place a huge drain on our relationship. We weren't prepared for the magnitude of the change."

"It was a lot of work starting a relationship with the kids," Gene said. "Possibly I tried too hard. I should have let things just evolve more."

Competition between children from each side of a new family and real or imagined favoritism by the stepparents are issues difficult to avoid. Neither are they easy to solve. But no matter what the issues are, all counselors say, "Work on being a couple first."

In keeping with this it's important to ask, "Why did I remarry?" Better still, ask it before remarriage. If you only want to provide your children with a new parent, problems will quickly surface. The marriage is the primary relationship; parenthood is secondary. As long as the marriage partners are united and strong, the children fare well and family tranquility has a chance.

INCEST: A SUBJECT NO ONE LIKES TO CONSIDER

As distasteful as the subject of incest may be, it merits a warning. Consider the words of family counselor Andre

Bustanoby: "Because stepbrothers and stepsisters are not related by blood, there is a greater likelihood of sex play in the blended family than in the natural family. But the guilt can be just as damaging.

"Stepparents and parents would do well to help the children cope with this temptation. I'm not talking about wild-eyed suspicion over the most innocent act or remark but a calm setting and enforcing of boundaries."

Bustanoby continues, "When the parents leave the children at home, an older woman might be invited to 'house sit.' Sexual decorum is important—no running around in underwear or bath towel. Also, after a certain hour everybody must be settled in his or her own room."[4]

Art Levine in an article in U.S. *News & World Report* wrote, "Tensions are often heightened by the budding sexuality of stepdaughters." He cites one girl who "would put on a fashion show" for her mother's date. Later, after her mom remarried, the girl apparently felt rejected and vowed that she would somehow get the new couple divorced.

The same article reported, "[Psychiatrist Clifford Sager] warns that remarried couples need to be sexually discreet, noting that an erotic atmosphere in remarriages can lead to a 'loosening of sexual boundaries.' Indeed, although only 8 percent of all children live with a stepfather, 30 percent of all cases of adult-child sexual abuse involve a stepfather."[5]

WORKING IT OUT

I asked several remarried couples, "If you were talking to a couple considering a marriage in which blending families would be necessary, what would you tell them?" The first recommendation was inevitably, "Go to family counseling before marriage."

A husband who hadn't been involved in counseling said wistfully, "It would be so helpful to have classes on blended families in advance."

One of the young couples interviewed has been involved in counseling for the family and individual children for several years after marriage. They had not had the advantage of premarital family counseling.

The length of time it takes for a blending family to develop some bonds and move into a comfort zone with one another varies greatly. It may be three years or, as with Darryl and Lisa, it may take twice that long.

The second major recommendation from young families was for both parties to sell their homes and get on neutral ground.

BLENDING AND BONDING CAN COME

Parents need to keep their commitment to each other and believe that, with counseling and a strong, personal faith, time is on their side. Then they can come through the blending experience to sunnier days, where their whole family is stronger and better-equipped for life.

After Lisa and Darryl had been married five years, Darryl's daughter told Lisa, "You know, this family is getting to be pretty neat. We don't fight as much as other families." As other children in the family were going into the military or off to school, the same girl remarked, "I always wanted to be an only child, but now I don't want anybody to leave!"

Lisa recalled: "I was so thankful that happened before

everybody left so that when they all come home they are glad to see each other. They didn't leave while they were still fighting and we were still fighting.

"In the process of healing we noticed first the two boys sticking together in arguments and the two girls on the other side instead of the kids from one parent pitted against those from the other. But it took a long time. When they were able to do that, we were able to go along with it. And the two of us healed.

"Now we can see that each of us has contributed to the lives of the other's children."

Darryl added, "She helped my daughter blossom. I've helped her daughter who is introvertish to learn some of my extrovert ways."

As if to put the final touch on their blending Lisa said: "When my daughter got married recently she struggled with who should give her away. She finally asked Darryl and felt comfortable with it. It was a beautiful symbol of her acceptance of him."

"And it was special for me," Darryl added, "She could have asked her uncle or anyone."

When a widow and widower remarry, they have one great advantage over couples who have lost a spouse by divorce. There are no personal intrusions by the former mate to unsettle the new relationship. There is no shuffling of children between different households. Nor is there the same financial strain from divorce settlements. After the grieving is over, a new life really can begin. And by the grace of God, the pain of blending can produce peace, joy, patience, and love.

WHY A BLENDED FAMILY IS UNIQUE:

1. Minor children impose a special set of needs and problems on a remarriage.
2. The blended family is a special entity itself; it is not the same as a traditional, first-marriage family.
3. Blending and bonding can take several years to achieve.
4. Family counseling is essential, but it is often overlooked in the usual premarital counseling. It is always wise to involve the children.

RESOURCES

The annual remarriage conference "Blended and Blessed" at the five-thousand-member New Hope Community Church, 11731 S.E. Stevens Road, Portland, OR, 97266, phone 503-659-5683, George Matteson, conference director. Presently this is the only conference of its kind in the U.S. Spanning three days on a November weekend, it touches all the basics on remarriage. While the majority attending are those wounded by divorce, much of the conference directly benefits the widowed.

11

Busting Ghosts and Merging Lives

While the dishwasher finished its clanking and went into the drying cycle, Emily fluffed her hair and checked her face in the mirror. Coat in hand, she started out the back door to her car, thankful there would be no dirty dishes begging for attention when she returned. Her husband, Ned, had left earlier for his church committee meeting.

As she walked down the three cement steps to the driveway, Emily felt a presence near her—the presence of a woman. It was as if someone else had used those stairs a thousand times before.

Emily felt shivers run down the back of her neck and from shoulder to shoulder. The foggy fall air muffled her own sounds. She couldn't understand the tinge of anger and resentment she felt. Even though she and Jenny had been the best of friends, this was too much. Of course she was imagining it. "I don't believe in ghosts," she said later. Yet it felt like Jenny's ghost was still hovering around the house. That ghost would have to go!

Determined not to tell Ned all the reasons why, Emily decided to ask him that night if they could sell the house and buy a new one. Jenny had lived in that house too long—too long for Emily to handle her feelings about that presence that kept coming back. You see, Jenny was Ned's first wife.

What Emily went through is not unique. It often happens to the remarried person who tries to move into a home where the previous spouse had lived for many years. Most couples aren't prepared to deal with the feelings that follow.

Darryl spoke of the ghost he competed with in the early years after he moved into Lisa's home: "There's a ghost here. With the kids, I'm kind of walking in Bart's [the deceased father's] shadow. Both her kids have said to me, 'If Bart were alive. . . .' He was a great guy, a friend of mine, but I felt his shadow get bigger and bigger. You forget all the bad things and remember the good. The shadow of a giant walks this house."

These *ghosts* are the internal feelings or reactions people have to external objects, occurrences or memories. Furniture, family pictures, flashbacks, handiwork, habits, cooking, decorating, comparisons, using the wrong name—any of these things can trigger such a response. A courting couple needs to be aware that some of these feelings will inevitably appear.

DEATH SCENE FLASHBACKS

Sometimes a specific scene recalls such a painful memory of the former spouse that an immediate change is necessary. Norene had such an experience: "David likes to lie down on the floor and have me walk on his back to straighten out his spine. But early in our marriage I had to let him know what that did to me. For instance, I might be fussing in the kitchen at bedtime. I'd come around a corner to the dimly lit bedroom. There he'd be lying on the floor!

"My heart would flip over because it would remind me of my first husband's death [she found him on the bedroom floor]. I finally said to David, 'You've got to tell me when you're going to do that. It takes me into the past and makes me think that maybe you're lying on the floor dead. It's scary to me!' So now he warns me."

If Norene had suppressed her feelings and been unwilling to let David know the pain his actions were inadvertently causing her, who knows what damage could have been done to her and to the marriage? But David and Norene had developed good communication patterns before their marriage, so she was able to let him know about the problem.

DON'T YOU KNOW MY NAME?

Ghosts of the past are often evoked unthinkingly by the mates themselves. An embarrassing moment for any couple is calling the new mate by the previous mate's name. Couples who had a previous marriage that lasted thirty years or more find it especially difficult. Most handle it well.

Nora admitted, "I've done it, and still do after twenty years. More often it comes to mind but doesn't come out. Roger has even introduced me by his first wife's name a couple of times. It doesn't bother either one of us. I suppose if there was jealousy . . . but I can't imagine it."

right to talk. That was part of our life. You can't wipe out
thirty or forty years of your life. It wasn't fair to just shut it off
because that was part of our healing—the healing that
comes from being able to talk to someone about those
things. Sometimes feelings have to get out. So we allow it."

YOU DON'T DO THINGS AS WELL

Comparing a new mate with a previous one can be
destructive to a marriage. Even though it may be without
malice or left unspoken, the results can still be negative. In
retrospect, Norene recognized something that happened in
her brief marriage after the loss of her first husband.

"I discovered when he moved into my home that
suddenly he wasn't like my deceased husband," she said.
"He didn't do things the same way. He didn't react the same
way. He didn't have the same habits or abilities. Where
before I had concentrated my total attention upon my fiance,
suddenly he wasn't measuring up very well to my former
husband.

"It was like everything positive about him turned negative once he moved into my home. I knew it wasn't all in him.
Something was happening in me. . . . The memory of my
deceased husband hadn't faded enough."

Aside from making mental comparisons, Norene had not
completed the grieving process. Steps omitted or not
completed in that process can come back to haunt a person's
new marriage.

Ned, who could have suffered by comparison to two
previous husbands said, "Emily has never even once indicated that her other husbands did something better than I

Busting Ghosts and Merging Lives

The confusion of names most often comes whe
who knew the previous spouses are visiting. "Peopl
our names when talking to us or about us, sometime
our former spouses' names with ours," Emily exp

Ned acknowledged that the two of them have the
slipped up at times: "When that happens, one persc
to give the other a funny look. Now we can laugh ab

While the mixing of names occurs "when the mout
into automatic," as one man put it, the problem c
avoided. Use the new mate's name in conversation whe
possible, and substitute the spouse's name for tern
endearment such as *honey*. This not only adds a tender t
to your use of your spouse's name, but it also helps re
your mind.

CONVERSATIONALLY SPEAKING

When conversation turns to former mates, it can rat
one or both of the new partners. Quoting the former ma
frequently or saying, "Jack and I used to go watch th
Dodgers every Thursday night during home stands," coul
say to the new partner that he isn't uppermost in mind.

Some couples try to eliminate all references to past
mates, but this can result in frustrating failure or guilt. Other
spouses have made the decision to put no restraint on their
conversations, including references to the former spouses.

Angie spoke of the understanding she and Eric have: "We
agreed that neither one of us would get upset if the other
one talked about the former mate. It was hard at times for me
to listen to him tell what 'she' did. It intimidated me, though
I know he did not mean it to. But the agreement gives us the

do. She's wonderful about that. She's thought it maybe, but she's never said it."

Nancy had been married a year or two before our interview. At age seventy-nine, she had this wisdom to offer: "It has not been any problem for me whatsoever. It's altogether new, a new love, new experience; there's no room for comparing. None. No room for jealousy. One of the most important things is to be absolutely mature. If we aren't mature by now, then there's no hope for us. And we can't afford to be touchy and selfish. All of that's out!"

Making comparisons may be the right thing to do when shopping, but they are counterproductive in a remarriage, especially if they are negative. Couples need to agree on how they will handle comparisons as they plan for marriage.

Most difficulties within any marriage have more than one solution. One may be best for one couple but not another. Here are some possible ways to avoid difficulty over partners using wrong names, bringing the former spouse into a conversation, or comparing one mate to another:

Agree in advance that there will be no anger or hurt in response when you are called by the wrong name. Be willing to laugh about it, if that's your personality, or agree to make extra effort not to commit the offense.

Pledge that you will be empathetic and responsive to the offender when any kind of reference is made to a past mate. Come to an understanding on how much you will allow past conversations and activities into present dialogue. Determine in advance if positive comparisons will be allowed or all comparisons are off limits. Most of all, agree to let your spouse express feelings about problems that come up, and be ready to work at changes you may need to make.

FACES ON THE WALL

Whether past family photographs project their active presence into the lives of the new couple depends much on where they are located, for this indicates their degree of importance. Also significant is whether there has been a mutual agreement about them and if there are other family members in the home.

When there are children living in the new household, even unmarried young adults, the previous family photos cannot be eliminated totally without damaging efforts to blend the two families. But there are solutions.

Certainly the spouses can display what they wish on their bedroom walls. But the bedroom is no place for pictures of former mates, or perhaps even nieces and nephews. Full sexual expression may not be possible if a former spouse or in-laws are watching from the dresser or the wall.

It may be tough to remove certain pictures. Ken recalled something in my interview with him and Nancy: "I remember one man who told me that the hardest thing he had to do when he married the second time was to take his first wife's picture down and put it away out of sight. And it was like that for me the first time I was widowed. But this time, no. I still have pictures put away in the bedroom I can go look at and she has pictures she can bring out. But to have them around to look at every day, no." He and Nancy agreed that it would be inappropriate.

A positive solution two couples found was to assemble a picture gallery of the two families, leaving out no one. One has it in their finished basement recreation room, the other in the main floor hallway. That way the children can maintain a sense of biological continuity and relationship. As one wife put it: "We have four generations on this wall. It's to help keep healthy memories alive and tie us all together."

AND THEN THERE'S THE HOUSE AND FURNITURE

Some mates find it easy, but most find it difficult to move into the house where the previous spouse lived. The quiver in Anna's voice testified to the depth of her feeling about moving in where two previous spouses had lived: "It was hard. It was really hard. It seemed like I couldn't cook, I couldn't do this or that. I was afraid to do things. Yorty said, 'If you don't want to live here we can sell the place and buy another.' But I didn't want to go through the problems of selling and buying," Anna survived those difficult days and assured me that now she felt more at home.

Nancy spoke in a light, cheerful way: "It doesn't bother me that his wife lived here. We have even merged our furniture and our dishes. We did get rid of some things, but we didn't buy one new item." She is one of the minority who, on her testimony and others' observations, appeared to have made the adjustment.

But another woman said, "I couldn't bear for us to share the bedroom in which my husband died."

A new spouse told his wife that every time he turned a corner he could see her husband somewhere in the house. It wasn't a vaporous ghost he was seeing. Rather, it was things his predecessor had built, things that bore his signature.

"It was a problem for me as a husband and father," said one man, "moving into a widow's home and adjusting. But she was considerate and sympathetic with me. However, she also had a standard of quality and care she wanted to keep in her house and I had to adjust to her feelings on this."

His wife added: "I've tried hard to make it *our* home, not *my* house."

"She had a rosebush out in back," continued the husband, "and I moved it. It really disturbed her. She didn't want that rose moved. So I was willing to put it back."

"And I felt terrible," the wife confessed.

An insignificant thing, an outside observer might say, but typical of the resistance to change human beings develop. It's the "little foxes that ruin the vineyards," as Solomon said.

Reasons why one mate moves into the other's house can include the desire for a child not to change schools, or that one spouse "just couldn't bear to move." Economics can also have a bearing, such as when one spouse owns a house and the other doesn't.

Darryl told me that moving into Lisa's house became an issue: "With the kids especially, you tend to claim owner-ship—'This is *our* house; you can't go into *my* room.' That's why my number one recommendation to a couple is to move to a neutral site where it's *everybody's* house. Then the kids can choose their own room. Even if you lose money on the sale of the home, in the long run it will be money well spent."

Lisa added, "For my kids, ownership extended even to towels and other things in the house. When they [Darryl and his children] moved in, they didn't even know where the pots and pans were—we did. It was that way with everything."

Some couples find that by redecorating or remodeling, the new mate can feel at home quickly. But others say that redecorating in no way camouflages the former "presence."

Sometimes the children, whether still at home or out on their own, feel the new mate has tried to take over their mother's or father's place in *their* home.

Most couples interviewed began their new marriage in different housing, as many experts recommend. And most who moved into the home of a former spouse admit that there can be severe complications.

Some solve the housing situation by selling their property and jointly purchasing a different home. Most widowed persons who own a home discover that it has sizeable equity or is owned outright.

Sometimes a couple rents out their homes and moves to a new house. If one spouse moved to a new house during his or her widowhood, that place often is seen as neutral ground. If the new couple did not own homes before their marriage, they can easily rent a different house or apartment.

New housing also brings decisions to make about furnishings. It is worth remembering that the older we get, the more important possessions can become. Even a Christian who professes to have his "treasures laid up in heaven," can become attached to things. This is usually because of their sentimental worth or simply because of the familiarity and sense of continuity they provide.

But what about those furnishings? Could they cause a tidal wave to swell on the matrimonial sea? Not quite. But where emotional attachment is involved, it doesn't take an earthquake to trouble the waters. Remember the man who told his wife that everywhere he turned he saw her deceased husband's signature on things in the home? That marriage didn't make it.

When both partners are willing to do anything to make

their marriage a new beginning, they make the necessary compromises about possessions. One man said: "We kind of mixed things together. Then we had a garage sale of the things we wanted least."

Another couple began their new life together with the husband giving all his furniture to his children. Then they moved her furniture in. So it became their home: her furniture, his house.

If one or both of the partners really cherish their furnishings or they don't have room to combine everything, there is another solution. Instead of giving the extra items to the children outright, try placing them on loan to the children, other relatives, or friends. It's surprising how items begin to lose their emotional tug when they are out of sight. A final decision will come more easily later.

Elsie related how she and Bob handled their furnishings when she moved into his house: "I wanted to be very sensitive to what was here and joining what I had with his. By his children making a list of what they wanted, it was easy for us to give them that. I could replace those pieces with mine. We changed upholstery—even on my furniture—and we remodeled the kitchen. I brought my bed for our bedroom and he accepted that."

Elsie had told Bob very directly that she preferred a different bed from his. Because she had been alone for ten years, she had one that had not been shared. And with the remodeling of the kitchen, Elsie could now call it her home too.

Elsie and Bob's actions illustrate one of the most sensitive areas in building a new life together. The bed from a previous marriage can be as inhibiting to sexual expression as the eyes of a former mate staring down from a photo on the dresser. Wisdom and sensitivity say, "Make some changes!"

If there is some item that is terribly important to a spouse, that person needs to make it known. By saying, "This is something I treasure and I'd like to see it out in the open," that spouse gives the other person the opportunity to let love rule. And love never fails—in anything.

WHAT SHOULD I REMEMBER?

1. Try to anticipate and eliminate any potential environment that would harbor "ghosts" your new mate might feel.
2. Recognize that both of you will probably revert to the previous spouse's name occasionally. Agree to laugh and try again.
3. Concur in advance how acceptable it will be to bring the former spouses into your conversation. By all means, avoid comparing mates.
4. Put away those photos of the former spouse, or if agreeable, establish a gallery of everyone from both families in a not-too-conspicuous place.
5. Neutral housing will probably have to be arranged and emotion-laden items of furnishing removed.

12

When It's Time
to Say "I Do"

"We'll hang you by your heels if you run off!" Those words could have been meant for a teenage daughter, but actually they were a friendly threat to Eric and Angie from their singles group. The group wanted to participate in the romantic saga in their midst. They wanted the couple to have a church wedding.

"I thought no one would really care about our wedding and was surprised to have people so excited," said Angie. "We had a stand-up ceremony after the regular evening church service. Our reception was the happiest I've ever been to."

So here's an early warning: When you decide to remarry, friends and family need to be considered. This is a major event for you and probably for them too. If your social circle has decreased with your increase in years, the number may be smaller, but the interest is probably still significant.

GET ME TO THE CHURCH ON TIME?

No typical wedding site emerged from the interviews with the widowed who remarried. What they did have in common was the absence of a large church wedding.

The most popular locations for weddings were home, outdoors, and small chapels. As with Eric and Angie, the church sanctuary is also possible when the wedding is linked with a church service or is an informal event at another time. If one of the new partners has never been married, especially if it's the bride, it is appropriate to have a full church wedding.

Kent and Donna were in their early thirties. She had never been married. The traditional elements of white gown, giving away, presents, and reception were all there. A large church full of guests and a big choir gave them support. Their personally composed vows expressed the significance of the event for each of them.

A full church wedding in a large sanctuary was also the choice of Everett and Ingrid. She had never been married before. Just after the exchange of marriage vows, Everett's two pre-school boys joined the wedding party on the platform.

Ingrid knelt and made this personally composed mothering vow to the two boys: "Terry and Larry, in the Bible in Deuteronomy, God tells me that as your mother I have a responsibility to teach you about his Word. It is also my responsibility to love and train you. I promise to do that for you. I will trust God to help your father and me to raise you the way He wants. I love you both." With a kiss for each boy, Ingrid stood up and rejoined Everett.

Other couples choose a Saturday afternoon ceremony like Roger and Nora's. "She didn't walk down the aisle but entered from a side room wearing a suit," Roger said. "There was an open invitation to the congregation and word of mouth to friends, with all invited to stay for the reception afterward."

Another couple, Loren and Esther, smiled as they told me, "We had our wedding right here in this living room."

The couples I interviewed selected their wedding location on the basis of sentiment, convenience, personal convictions, size of the wedding party, and number of guests expected. Most couples were interested in a low-key occasion; some wanted it quite private. Others wanted to accommodate a larger circle of friends and family.

"Our wedding was here in the backyard," one woman explained. "Most of our families were here, quite a few friends and all the pastoral staff from our church. That meant a lot to me."

Still another couple had their wedding in a condominium clubhouse.

WHO WILL ATTEND?

Attendance at the ceremony varies from just the couple, two witnesses, and the officiant, to a chapel or sanctuary well-filled with friends.

With one exception, none of the couples surveyed indicated the use of formal invitations. An informal invitation issued through word of mouth or printed in the church bulletin or newsletter is effective. Or the couple, close friends, or family members may write a personal note to those they specifically desire to be in attendance.

One younger bride used home-printed invitations with a drawing her children could color. By doing some of the art work, the children felt this was their wedding too, when they would get a new daddy.

Most couples included older children who lived within traveling distance in their wedding plans. Sometimes, if relationships were strained, the children did not attend.

"We had a quiet wedding," said one man. "The minister wouldn't marry us unless we called all the children on both sides. We did that, but none of them came to the wedding. There was only my sister, her husband, and my mother that came. Some couldn't come because of distance. But we did feel badly because the only congratulation card we got was from my daughter. Otherwise nobody acknowledged our wedding. Later, my brother and his wife had a gathering for us and I've always been thankful for that."

With this incident in mind, I have a word for adult children who are distanced from their family or disapprove of their widowed parent's plans to remarry: Whatever the cause of your emotional separation or disapproval, it is never right to withdraw from a parent at this time. If you feel it is appropriate, express your opinions ahead of time. But if the wedding still goes forward, be there or be supportive in some other way. The marriage might work out in spite of your reservations. If it doesn't, you want to be in a position where you will be able to help your parent pick up the pieces.

Nancy, at seventy-nine, was as bubbly as a college girl

about her wedding day: "It was a great occasion. My family and his family were marvelous. We used every single one we could in the wedding. His son was best man and my daughter was matron of honor. Another son gave me away and a third son performed the ceremony with my brother assisting. The grandkids messed up the car. All of the family were there. We felt very strongly that it should be low-key and not a big church affair, just a family wedding."

Like Nancy and Ken, most couples deeply desired their children's presence and participation in the wedding party. Not only did they want them at the wedding, but they wanted them to stand with them in the ceremony. In addition to providing public demonstration of their support, children in the bridal party give continuity as the past merges into the future.

AND THE BRIDE WORE ...

In keeping with the generally informal tone of most of the weddings, the brides I interviewed did not wear white or a formal wedding dress of any color. The only exceptions were when the bride had not been previously married. The brides usually wore a street-length dress, and the grooms a business suit or even less-formal attire.

Regardless of what the bride wears, giving her away is taboo, according to George W. Knight in *The Second Marriage Guidebook*.[1] However, some of the older widows preferred being given away. In some instances it may be because of the less independent stance of their generation. More often it is for the reassurance, approval, and encouragement it tends to give.

Whatever the reason, most Americans feel the freedom to innovate or to do what makes them feel most comfortable. So go ahead and be creative. It's your wedding.

WHAT? ANOTHER TOASTER?

George Knight wrote that it is best not to expect wedding gifts and that they should be discouraged. However, a lay counselor told me that gifts at the time of the second marriage should not be discouraged. She says they help to acknowledge the new union.

Even Amy Vanderbilt refrains from giving a definitive ruling on the question of gifts: "The bride who has been married before, whether she is widowed or divorced, technically should not expect wedding gifts, although in actual practice many people do give them."[2] Vanderbilt agrees that if one of the couple has not been married before, then gifts are more appropriate.

Depending on the age, need, or wishes of the couple, the question of gifts can be settled as seems best in each situation. Especially when two households are being merged, there isn't the need for the usual items. If family or friends feel some gift would be appropriate, their creative sense will help them settle on some small item. Sometimes a group-gift will be in order. Love will always meet the needs of the moment.

FATHER DOESN'T PAY THIS TIME

No wedding is without some expense. Who pays for it this time? It's not up to the bride's parents, although if they are living, they may provide a helpful gift. Unless there is a great difference in the financial resources of the new partners, the wedding expenses are split between them. The couple should have learned from experience that mortgaging the future by splurging on the present is never worth it. Do what you can comfortably afford.

The expenditures related to the wedding day or already advanced for a honeymoon are not normally large enough to be significant. But remodeling your present home or purchasing a different house, or signing a lease agreement can create added pressure to go ahead with the marriage. It may seem wrong to waste the money, so any late doubts about the wisdom of the marriage may not be taken seriously.

If either party has questions about the wisdom of proceeding with the new marriage, you should reconsider or even cancel the plans. Far better to risk losing some money than to enter a marriage about which you have reservations.

It is worth remembering that almost every bride or groom who takes marriage seriously can have last minute jitters or doubts. These are normal. A friend may urge you to cast doubts aside as unimportant at this stage. But if you cannot sort out normal jitters from legitimate doubts, talk with a trusted, objective counselor. Whatever happens, don't let money control your decisions.

NOT NIAGARA FALLS AGAIN!

Almost ninety percent of the couples I surveyed had a honeymoon. Some honeymoons were a week or less in length, while others lasted two or three weeks. There were elaborate trips to the ocean with sunset walks on the sand

and also cross-country expeditions. There were also simple trips to a nice motel or hotel across town.

What is good advice for young couples about sex on the honeymoon is even more significant the second time around. Be very patient with one another.

So what if there is not a completed act the first time when both are overly tired? This is no time for an ego trip or the demand to meet predetermined performance standards. Let time and patience give the freedom to function adequately. And remember, demonstrative affection always helps to take care of sexual needs. If the couple has carefully discussed their expectations earlier, these days should go well.

Some newlyweds will joke about being on a continuous honeymoon, but that's stretching the meaning of the word. Life isn't that way. Lance and Rana, however, deliberately worked at keeping the honeymoon spirit alive. He told me: "We celebrated our anniversary every week until the fiftieth week, so we could have a fiftieth wedding anniversary. We took the kids along for our fiftieth celebration. Then we started celebrating the months."

If you have been deprived of a golden wedding anniversary because you're middle-aged or older, take a tip from that couple and keep celebrating this new experience.

If God should bring another person into your later life, your time together can well be some of the best years you have known.

REVIEWING SOME DO'S BEFORE THE "I DO"

1. Do remember that other people are sincerely interested and need to be considered when you plan your
   wedding.

2. Do choose the setting for your wedding that satisfies
   your social, financial, and spiritual needs.

3. Do plan for a honeymoon, that initial adjustment
   period, of whatever length you can afford.

13

Roof Off, Walls Down

The phrase *Roof Off, Walls Down* is part of a Ugandan proverb. It's a prescription for good communication. In the Ugandan culture, it means "nothing hidden from God or people." While communication is important before marriage, it is vital after the wedding to solidify a good, peaceful relationship.

Bert and Elsie expressed the spirit of "roof off, walls down," when I asked if they had any final counsel for new partners. Bert said: "Go into it with as near total openness as possible. It didn't take us long to be that way. But I can understand that with two people who did not know each other or if their kids did not know each other, it would take longer. The thing we have done well is that we started from the beginning to be open with each other. I told her that I can deal with anything that is out on the table one way or another. But I have a hard time dealing with hidden agendas."

Elsie interrupted by saying, "He insists on knowing where I am emotionally. He allows me to be open."

"If I see her clouded," Bert explained, "I will say, 'I can't wait very long for you to tell me what's bothering you.' I can change almost anything if I understand."

Unmet expectations in recreation, money, sex, or any other dimension of living can provoke problems in relationships. If we don't talk about our expectations with our mate, whose fault is it if they are unmet? Openness works both ways: Your spouse understands you better, and you are more likely to have your needs met.

SHRED THAT HIDDEN AGENDA

"Holding on to a hidden agenda is a sure road to a quick divorce after remarriage," wrote Mel Krantzler in *Learning to Love Again*. "Nothing undermines the trust of the other party in the relationship more than the hiding of issues that should be discussed."[1]

Whether it is a secret agenda an executive has in the boardroom, a politician's real plans not told to his constituency, or one party entering a marriage with hidden goals, a hidden agenda is basically deception or manipulation at work. Marriage calls for complete trust and openness. If these are absent, little is left.

Sometimes a hidden agenda may mean refusing or neglecting to talk about certain subjects during marriage in order to gain a personal end. I read about one remarried widow who refused to collect the interest on some bonds she owned because she didn't want her new husband to know she had them. She died without ever gaining any benefit from them!

At other times, a hidden agenda may mean talking about a subject or proposing solutions that will gain your objectives at the expense of your unsuspecting mate. Personal integrity and honesty should rule out the hidden agenda. If it is written but carried in an inside pocket, shred it; if it is unwritten and carried in the mind, purge it.

COMMUNICATION

One marriage and family counselor says, "Communication is to love what blood is to life."[2] Without blood we die; if there is not genuine communication, love will die and the marriage with it.

The communication normal to modern marriages has not been commonly practiced by older couples. This is not to say they do not value conversation. Rather, suppression, especially of negative feelings, was more the rule. Younger couples usually prefer openness and the full expression of all feelings.

There are not just generational differences in how couples handle communication. Individuals of all ages differ in their ability to communicate. Some people try to solve problems by ignoring them. Others delight in head-on collisions with issues or people. Some people should get Oscars for effectively (but often disastrously) hiding their feelings. Still others explode emotionally all over the landscape, spattering everyone in view.

Far better to allow for and deal with emotions. Often, a

question or comment such as, "It sounds like you really hated that" (or you are really angry, or you feel very sad, or you truly miss him) will allow for the constructive expression of emotions.

WE THINK, SEE, AND HEAR DIFFERENTLY

Each of us comes to a situation with a different set of experiences, relationships, and environments. Therefore our perceptions of what is said or the circumstance of the moment can vary widely. The key is to discover how your spouse sees what you see or hears what you say. Then cross-check to see if you are hearing correctly what your spouse is saying.

One way is to ask questions, lots of them. These questions are not just for information about what your spouse is thinking. They are to find out if he or she has heard what you actually said. It also helps to repeat what you heard your spouse say to you. Then ask "Honey, did I understand you correctly?"

Hearing words is not important; understanding what someone means is. We can't be sure that we understand someone unless we listen carefully, ask questions, and check to make sure we are hearing correctly.

The Bible provides some good reminders about the importance of listening: "He who answers before listening— that is his folly and his shame" (Proverbs 18:13). "Everyone should be quick to listen, slow to speak and slow to become angry" (James 1:19).

Esther talked about how she and Loren communicate when they get angry with each other: "When I get a little angry, I try to calm myself down and not say anything for quite a while. I have a quick reaction and I've found that if I keep quiet for a while and think about it, I'll be more sensible when we talk.

"Or if I've made a decision regarding one of my children, he may not say anything for a while. Then he will comment, 'I think maybe you'd better reconsider that.' And we'll talk about the whole thing and why. Often I change my mind. We are good communicators. We spend a lot of time talking."

When I asked Darryl and Lisa how well they communicate, Lisa said: "That's one of the things our family counselor had to work with us on. We became too tense and argumentative. We learned how to discuss the problems we had with the children and talk through our differences in handling them. It became possible to come to a midpoint so that each of us was comfortable in each situation we had to deal with. But it was important for us to talk together first and then go unitedly to the kids. Each of us had been so different in handling disciplinary problems before we remarried."

Darryl added, "If we had taken family counseling before the marriage it could have sped up the blending time by two years or more. Sometimes we thought we wouldn't make it. We care for each other greatly, but there were times when the conflict was so overpowering that the caring was lost."

There is conflict in every marriage. You had it in your first; you'll have it in your second. How we handle the conflicts is the important thing.

In the boxing ring you win, lose, or draw. But in emotional bouts you can run away; give in; disregard others so you win what you want; or develop good communication skills to resolve the conflicts for everyone's best interest.

One way to improve communication is to provide opportunities for it. Such planning does not restrict spontaneous moments, but it guarantees there will be times to talk.

Some couples schedule a weekly breakfast at their favorite restaurant where, over waffles and coffee, they can unhurriedly talk about whatever is on their mind. Others find that late evening before bedtime becomes a routine time for significant conversation. Subjects for discussion are not limited to problems, but include hopes, dreams, goals, fears, questions, and expressions of concern for each other.

The important thing is to talk. Just as physical wounds left untended will likely become worse, other needs can also fester from neglect.

COMMUNICATION VERSUS SPILLING YOUR GUTS

Concern for openness is not an invitation to spill your guts thoughtlessly. Communication prior to or during marriage means an honest effort to help your spouse understand what you think or feel or have experienced. It requires you to say no more and no less than what is necessary to bring two lives into harmony.

Elaine Mynatt wrote in *Remarriage Reality*: "Professionals vary on the degree to which spouses should tell each other all the dark secrets of their pasts or the fantasies of the present, and individuals differ as to how much they want to know. Even when the spouse begs to know every juicy detail, the facts of the matter may shock or hurt. . . .

"Certainly any major event in your life should be revealed

to your spouse, preferably before marriage. If you've been incarcerated, mentally ill, sterilized, alcoholic, had an illegitimate baby, or carry a latent disease, by all means admit it before the relationship becomes permanent."[3]

That author gave generally sound advice. However, one counselor on a church staff cautioned: "You needn't disclose anything that would destroy the relationship. . . . You don't want to share things that would be hurtful to the mate. On the other hand, you don't want to have a lack of integrity. Share the things that need to be shared. Complete openness on what you and your former mate did is not necessary."

One general rule is to be sure to talk about any negative event in your life which will likely come up anyhow or which, if discovered accidently by your spouse, would create problems. Providing information before the remarriage gives your prospective mate an opportunity to make informed choices. No one likes unhappy surprises.

PAST PAIN CAN STILL HURT

Sometimes an event or a conversation will bring to the surface a long-buried negative experience. You forgot about it or thought it could have no bearing on your remarriage. Yet something happens, triggering old feelings. Norman and Nan had lost mates by death and the rejection of divorce. Nan told how some past experiences affected their new life together:

> When I go to the store I like to look at the magazines and read the food labels and take my time about it. When I came home one time, Norman was sitting there with the

most awful look on his face. He asked me, "Where have you been!" I couldn't understand what he was thinking.

Finally, as we talked about it, I realized how much he had been hurt and not recovered from the past. He thought he was going through the same thing again. |Nan's longer-than-usual absence caused Norman to think back to the unfaithfulness of his previous wife.|

Another time it was something from my past. Norman asked me if he could go shopping with me. But that had been a bad experience for me in my first marriage. My husband would go with me. He would hurry me along, pretending outwardly that everything was okay. But he would take my arm and intentionally pinch it hard as we walked along fast. I got so I couldn't make up my mind what to buy or do anything.

So when Norman went with me I guess I thought I would go through the same thing again. When I asked him if I should get this or that he would say, "I don't care." I couldn't cope with this totally different attitude until we talked it out and he realized what had happened to me. So it is those previous painful experiences you bring into later marriages that cause problems too. But openness and communication on the deeper levels resolve things. We learned to be that way.

Norman and Nan have a better-than-average chance at a good marriage because they have learned to communicate. You can too. Books on communication and problem-solving continue to roll off the presses. Check your library and bookstores.

Silent Sams and zip-lipped Janes create unhappiness and even disaster in marriages. On the other hand, genuine and complete self-disclosure before marriage will help tie a ravel-proof wedding knot. It takes more than "I do" to have a wedding and build a marriage. Allow the time and make the effort to communicate—perhaps even more than for your first marriage. The payoff will last the rest of your life.

REVIEWING SOME WORTHY GOALS
AFTER YOUR WEDDING:

1. Borrow or buy a book or two dealing with communication in marriage.
2. Check your listening skills. Using the suggestions given, see how well you are really hearing others.
3. Try to live with "roof off, walls down," yet don't say things that would hurt your partner or cut future communication.
4. Make certain there are specific times when unhindered conversation and communication can take place.

14

Walking Together

He possessed only a few sycamore-fig trees and some ugly, dachshund-like sheep, valuable for the excellence of their wool. His hands, calloused and scarred from work in rocky soil, masked the role for which he is remembered. His name? Amos. His role? God's prophet with a message for Israel.

If two people were seen walking together in the desolate regions around Tekoa where Amos lived, it was assumed they had met by appointment rather than chance. That's the image Amos had in mind when he asked his rhetorical question, "Do two walk together unless they have agreed to do so?"

While Amos was pointing out problems in Israel, failure to achieve a united vision can also wreak havoc in a marriage. How do the remarried avoid this danger? How do they learn to walk together?

I asked remarried couples what they had learned about joining forces. Their comments provide valuable insights not only about a couple's day-to-day walk together, but also about their relationship with God. They talked about compatibility, flexibility, compromise, love, friendship, and the Lord's will. They also identified common problem areas that need attention.

THE RELATIVES

Family hurts can often be greater in extent and intensity for the widowed than for the never-married. One reason is that most of the time the widowed must deal with adult children, both theirs and their partners. Those children can be strong adversaries.

In addition, new mates bring long-held habits, opinions, likes, and dislikes which impact the children and other relatives. Changes and adjustments are not made easily. Any difficulties between a husband and wife may be amplified by the relatives.

Evelyn and Larry found that some of their children not only ignored their wedding, but also made life difficult after the event. Larry's daughter wouldn't even acknowledge their marriage. The only contacts were what Evelyn called "bad" letters. Larry responded by writing to his daughter and telling her, "If you can't accept my wife, you can't accept me." The situation reached an emotional stalemate.

There were also problems with Evelyn's children. Her son, Don, invited Larry out for pizza. Instead of a casual conversation, Larry found he had been ambushed. Don began making accusations about the vacation trailer and house his mother owned. Sharp words ended the conversation, and Larry walked out. Don later accepted assurances that the property still belonged to his mother, and the relationship healed.

Because of these experiences, Evelyn had strong words of warning for the widowed who are contemplating remarriage: "Don't get married until you meet the entire family! Get their reactions. I think some people have miserable marriages just because the families do things that make it so for them."

COMPATIBILITY: BEND OR BREAK

Some of the mix of compatibility includes flexibility and compromise. Compromise can be a dirty word where moral values are concerned. However, in human relations it has been well said that, "When we're in our twenties we refuse to compromise; in our thirties we'll think about it; in our forties we may do it; by the time we are fifty we realize that's what life is all about."

Ed realized how important compromise was in his marriage to Tammy: "If a person is like I am, who always thinks he's right, make sure you don't get someone else like that. You need to be flexible. Just like this afternoon, I was trying to tell Tammy how to prune the roses."

Tammy replied, "I told him that if I was going to do it, I was going to do it my way."

"See?" Ed said. "There's no use butting your heads together about the roses. Just back off!"

If compatibility is your goal, then be flexible. Being

willing to give in or "back off," as Ed put it, gives people the ability to compromise. And compromise leads to compatibility. Bend, so you don't break in the storm. Give, so you don't lose over the long haul. Otherwise, you may face constant misery in your marriage.

BECOMING BEST FRIENDS

When happily married people speak of their relationship, they frequently say, "He [or she] is my best friend." They truly enjoy doing things together. They like each other's company and conversation. They like each other for who they are—not for what they do for each other. Most important, deep friendship allows real love to develop.

The detailed process of becoming best friends varies. When I talked with Ken and Nancy, Ken told me: "We have continued to talk a lot in our marriage just as we did in our dating. We keep getting to know each other better all the time. It's the shared conversations that help develop mutual respect, understanding, appreciation, and our great friendship."

Others find that it is in doing things together, enjoying each others' interests, or sharing the work that their friendship is enhanced.

Sharing responsibilities in the home is not an idea invented by married yuppies. "I think being willing to share the work helps a lot," said Eric, a remarried senior. "I know some couples where the man never does a thing, just doesn't help. But we share everything."

One lay counselor cautioned against too much togetherness when she said: "There is a need for them to have activities of their own. Always being together can stifle personal growth. We need to grow all our lives. All human beings are gifted differently and need to exercise their gifts."

By continually developing our own gifts, hobbies, or knowledge of what's going on in the world, we can remain interesting to our best friend. Reading and conversation with others helps to keep us mentally fresh.

One couple recommended that retired marrieds, whose entire days may be spent within fifty feet of each other, should have more than minimum housing space, if at all possible. They can then escape to their own private work or play space. Later they will come back together, better able to meet each other's needs.

UNFAILING LOVE

Incurable romantics, while not always understanding what love is, unquestionably agree that it brings some obvious changes. A new look on the face, a quickened step, a certain confusion, more rapid pulse, more attention to grooming, and an embarrassed smile when a special friend is mentioned may all be signs of romantic love.

But unfailing love is that which goes beyond friendship love or passionate love, both of which are appropriate in their place. It is a love every person and every marriage craves, knowingly or not. Such love is illustrated in God himself.

When we read "God so loved the world that he gave his one and only Son" and then think of what happened to that Son, we realize how costly love can be. It means, as illustrated by Jesus, putting someone else's interests and welfare first. It fills life's potholes. It's the glue in commitment. It sustains while caring for someone who has a lengthy illness.

God expects us to show unfailing love to others. Jesus said, "My command is this: Love each other as I have loved you" (John 15:12).

It was this kind of love Nora spoke of when she said, "Love each other! I love him with all my heart. I tell Roger that. We tell each other every day. I thank the Lord for him."

Most people can't imagine a marriage without some level of love. However, some widowed persons remarry for financial security, companionship, or some other personal priority. But without God-like love, any marriage is on thin ice. The apostle Paul knew what he was talking about when he wrote, "And now these three remain: faith, hope and love. But the greatest of these is love" (1 Corinthians 13:13).

THE SPIRITUAL BOND

The great majority of couples I interviewed said the spiritual bond was most important for their marriage. All made some profession of faith; some were more open or mature in their faith than others. Though they could accept someone from another church, they wanted to be certain their partner had a personal relationship with Jesus Christ. Even so, there are always varying depths of commitment or different patterns of spiritual growth.

If faith in God is valued more than anything else, how are lives blended? What role do the Bible, church attendance and service, personal or family devotions, and related issues play in married life?

Achieving unity in faith and practice takes time. Significant conversations with your spouse about how you came to Christ and your own spiritual struggles and victories can build a foundation. Also discuss ideas from sermons and Bible studies, or debate ethical issues raised in the news.

Because Bert and Elsie lived about fifty miles apart before their marriage, they let AT&T help them begin building their lives together, including accountability to each other in their devotional life.

"Since we've been married," Bert said, "we have continued a pattern of devotions together, even in bed with coffee. We are free from little kids bouncing on the bed and all that. We read and pray together in a way that maybe neither of us was able to do with our other spouse. That's intensely satisfying."

Ken and Nancy had been in marriages that had given each a lifetime accustomed to worship in the home. "It's just so natural to have prayer and read the Scripture together right after the evening meal while we're still together at the table," Nancy explained. "We look forward to it every day."

Most couples agree that family devotions is one of the most important disciplines in their lives together. However, even great desire for regular devotions does not mean it can be accomplished easily. Darryl and Lisa, who each brought two children to their marriage, mentioned a struggle many families can identify with.

"My family had always had devotions together and was organized, knowing when we would do what," Lisa said. "But this has been such a bedlam-type thing that to get everyone together for devotions just didn't happen, though occasionally we had family meetings and prayer."

On the other hand, worship and participation in church life sometimes takes discussion and creativity more than anything else. Ned and Emily said the question of which church to attend was the most difficult thing they had to face.

"I've been involved in my church for over thirty years and she'd been involved in hers at least that long," Ned explained. "I wrestled with this. I didn't think it would be right for me to say, 'You have to leave your church and come with me.' I'm not sure that what we decided would work for a younger person. But it works for us.

"Our normal plan is to go to my church Sunday morning and hers in the evening and on Wednesdays. We each have two church families now and feel at home in each other's congregation. She supports her church financially and I support mine. It was a tough decision, but my pastor felt it was a reasonable solution."

About 25 percent of couples I surveyed decided to learn from each other's heritage and help in each other's churches when possible. With their great concern for spiritual unity, Ned, Emily, and others, did not bargain away their faith when they married. Instead, their faith bonded them.

Paul's caution to marry only "in the Lord," that is, when both know they are in personal union with Jesus Christ, was obviously followed in the lives and counsel of most of the remarried couples I surveyed. Their journey together was made possible by working through many issues, having a commitment to each other, and sharing a commitment to God.

WALKING TOGETHER IN MARRIAGE INCLUDES:

1. Continuing to cultivate each other's families.
2. Developing the art of compromise.
3. Becoming better or best friends, yet allowing each other space.
4. Knowing and sharing the love of God even more.
5. Practicing your worship and devotional life together.

15

The Church
and the Widowed

About two miles from my desk is the five-thousand-member New Hope Church of Portland, Oregon. It advertises itself as having ninety need-meeting ministries. Few congregations can match its breadth of activity, including programs that specifically benefit the widowed. Most congregations have fewer members, thus limiting the personnel and funds available to support such work. Other churches suffer from spiritual cataracts.

Yet God's compassionate concern for the widowed can't be missed. In the Hebrew family structure, the oldest son was responsible for his widowed mother. If there were no children, then the deceased husband's brother was to marry the widow so that she could have children, thereby preserving the husband's name and inheritance. This provision was extended to distant relatives of the same line, as illustrated in the story of the widow Ruth's marriage to Boaz.

In the changed cultural setting of the early church, neglect of widows caused some organizational changes. There were no pensions or government provisions for those widows. Ultimately the responsibility for their care fell on the church family, although any immediate relatives were also expected to step in (1 Timothy 5:4).

A compassionate concern for the widowed is still expected and needed today. That comfort can take any form of assistance for people in emotional, financial, social, psychological, or spiritual distress.

To better understand the feelings and needs of the widowed in the local church, let's look at some specific concerns they raised and consider possible solutions.

Casual Dating. The teenage-like attitude of some fellow church-goers toward casual dating bothered one person I interviewed. "That 'ahhh,' with a roll of the eyes that has you all but married," she complained. "Or if you happen to sit in church by some eligible person of the opposite sex, people fall all over themselves jumping to conclusions."

A man said, "I needed companionship . . . friendship. I'd like to have just taken someone out for pancakes, but you can't do it without people linking you together."

Solution. Church leaders can remind the widowed that these situations are generally well-intentioned, happy reactions by other members of their spiritual family. These people may be overly solicitous, but they are also caring friends who want to be part of the drama. Some may have difficulty in keeping a discreet distance or withholding comment. And what is irritating to one single may be welcomed by another.

Second, through consistent teaching and counseling, leaders can help the congregation to be more sensitive to efforts by the widowed to meet their own social needs. Greater sensitivity should result in greater restraint in attitudes and comment to or about those dating.

However, everyone should remember that happy interest can degenerate into idle gossip. Thoughtful members who avoid kidding and unnecessary comment endear themselves to singles. Periodic re-emphasis on the biblical teaching of James about the power of the tongue and the necessity to keep a tight rein on it will help answer singles' concerns.

Many singles will only want social dating and companionship. Some widows will prefer to find their social fulfillment in a circle of other widows who understand and can be supportive. The broader family needs to be made aware that remarriage is not the only option for the widowed or the never married. Singleness can be a productive, happy life at any age whether by choice or through lack of opportunity to marry.

Fair-Weather Friends. One active churchwoman said: "I don't know how it is for men, but women can be real close to couples before loss of a mate. Then afterward, they drop you. You are a fifth wheel then. It seems like the women may fear you're going to come after their husbands. I don't know why they act that way. I think people should be considerate of the person who is left alone."

This woman felt a close relationship with others in her church during the illness and death of her spouse. But after the loss, her social contact suffered. Most widowed persons report that after the first few weeks, contacts dwindle and they are left to themselves.

Solution. Through prayer groups, home Bible studies, Sunday school classes, the church paper, and other means, church leaders can provide teaching for the congregation about grief and how to respond to the grieving. Most people don't realize that the normal recovery time is about a year, and even longer for some people. With our fast-paced, complex lives, we easily forget the intense loss a grieving person is facing.

When President Franklin D. Roosevelt's mother died, he wore a black armband for many months. Aside from honoring the memory of the dead, the armband said to both friend and stranger that the wearer was still in a time of grieving. It helped prevent thoughtless remarks that could needlessly wound the grieving person. It communicated, "This person still needs emotional support."

We no longer have such visible signs of a person's loss, so how much more important it is for church staff, support groups, and friends to remind each other of a widowed person's need for continued contact with others.

It's easy to assume someone else is being supportive of the widowed person after the first few days; what is everyone's opportunity to minister can become no one's responsibility. Is a layleader responsible for that person? Are there one or more support groups in the church that will maintain contact with the grieving person? If not, now is the time to develop a system for future ministry.

There are, however, some sensitive people who have a broad view of family life in the church. For example, one widow said that after the sudden death of her husband, four other couples whom they had been friends with became her strength. The men helped her to have healthy male friendships. In too many instances the widow becomes isolated from interaction with men and the counsel they can give.

A widower can be even more isolated because men often do not have close male friends with whom they talk freely about their feelings and problems. So both the widow and widower need a church with a caring ministry.

Leaders can teach members of the church family to avoid gratuitous remarks made out of ignorance and embarrassment. Rather than tell the widowed to call the church for help whenever they need it, how much better it would be to have people visit them in their homes and observe or ask what needs to be done over the weeks and months. As the Nike sports shoe slogan says, "Just do it!"

Another comment better left unsaid is, "I know just how you feel." Even a person who has grieved probably does not know the exact dynamics of another individual's loss. A person who had a well-concealed, miserable marriage could experience mixed feelings of guilt and liberation. Being a quiet, sensitive listener and responding appropriately to what is heard is always safer and more helpful.

Self Isolation. The widowed sometimes sentence themselves to self-confinement. Many widows feel that they cannot go alone to banquets or other events which are predominantly attended by couples. It is almost as though their social life ended when their husband died.

Solution. How a widowed person resolves grief is an intensely personal process. It must be worked out in the inner recesses of the soul through interaction with God. But grief resolution also has social implications.

Other people who have been touched by the deceased go through a grieving process as well. They need contact with the one who was closest to that person. The surviving partner's complete withdrawal from social events denies that contact and also leaves the widow or widower emotionally vulnerable to extended or distorted grieving. The church leaders and family can gently urge involvement in a grief recovery program and help the widowed move back into social activity gradually.

One woman recounted: "The month after my first husband died, a couple called up and wanted to take me to dinner and the group fellowship. It never entered my mind that I couldn't go because I was a widow and they were couples. We were a group of friends."

This woman was determined to remain socially active. The church can help communicate this spirit and pull the widowed into the mainstream. It can provide support groups of widowed persons ministering to other persons and encourage couples to include the widowed in social events. The church can also offer the widowed opportunities to serve on boards and committees as their healing progresses.

Singles' Social Life. Despite the desirability of integrating widowed persons into the total church social life, they still have their own specific needs as singles. "I think the church could stress activities for the single, mature adult," one remarried widower said. "We have singles in their fifties who are totally neglected."

Solution. Because most churches in the United States are small, social activities for singles are ordinarily found in larger congregations and mega-churches. If widowed persons in smaller churches desire the fellowship of other singles or want other kinds of specialized ministries for themselves, their pastors will need to unselfishly encourage them to seek such support in trans-denominational situations.

Unintentional Hurts. Without thinking how worship practices affect different social groups, worship leaders plan services with married people and families in mind. "You don't realize this until it hits you between the eyes as a newly-widowed person," one individual commented. "For instance, when serving communion, sometimes all families are invited to come forward together and receive it. Where does that leave the singles? Or on Mother's Day it's, 'Well, husbands, put your arm around your wife.' These things in the church which are meant to help unite couples and families leave the widowed hurting."

Solution. Pastors can be more sensitive to singles and more creative in how they address their congregation on these special days. Perhaps there isn't a need to emphasize families at communion; that experience is a very personal act. Pastors may be torn between their desire to reinforce the disintegrating nuclear family and their broader responsibility to the larger church family.

The nuclear family is only part of the community of believers. Each has its role, but they are not identical. When pastors clearly teach the differences and yet endeavor to strengthen both, confusion between the two will cease.

Why not recognize both nuclear families and singles at different times? Emphasize our personal relation with the Lord, or how Jesus ministered to individuals, or the unique contributions singles make to the life of the church. At other times give special recognition and encouragement to widows. This is certainly biblical.

DEVELOPING A MINISTRY TO THE WIDOWED

Here's a broad sketch for ministry to the widowed by the local church. Preachers, teachers, counselors, care groups, social life leaders, and some of the widowed themselves can be the ones to implement the action plans.

One. Grief therapy is probably the most neglected area of the church's ministry to the widowed. The minister to senior adults at First Baptist Church of Modesto, California, told me about his church's program especially for the newly widowed: "Most cities and counties have some kind of secular program for the widowed, but not the churches," he said. "In our city I don't know of any church besides our own that has a ministry to widowed singles. Long before anything is done on remarriage, some kind of ministry to the newly widowed must happen. This allows you to have some input to their lives while getting them through the grief process."

That minister strongly encourages a twelve- to eighteen-month involvement in "The Upholders," a group that brings healing and mutual support from others who are widowed. The group helps the widowed to avoid making rash decisions and to face the many adjustments that are ahead. It also provides the church a way to reach into the community.

"I was reading the obituaries," the same minister told me a little later. "It grieved me that so many died and left a mate with no church affiliation. I consulted a college professor who herself had gone through this experience. I asked her to write a letter to those survivors expressing the church's concern, inviting them to inquire about our special support group for the widowed. The response has snowballed."

He said many people from the community have been

drawn into "The Upholders" where they have received the care they needed in their bereavement.

This program can be adapted to almost any church of medium or large size with a ministry to mature adults or the widowed. By ministering during the initial loss, the church earns the opportunity to help again when the widowed decide to marry.

Another person who ministers to single adults in a large church takes a different approach. She said she did not use support groups for the widowed because the groups tended to keep the widowed from moving on with life. She prefers to get the widowed integrated in the life of the church.

Two. Teach the adult congregation about loneliness, remarriage, and biblical perspectives on both older people and the widowed.

"People become impatient toward the grieving," observed Pauline, a widow at forty. "There are those in church who are uncomfortable with me that I'm still grieving over my loss. I have been going on with my life: working, going to school to better prepare myself for the future, and caring for my children. What they don't realize is that church was our family time. We were always there as a family. Now we aren't. Tell them not to forget the important holidays and anniversaries of the loss. Make a note of them. Mentioning them lets a person know that others are truly thinking of them."

Three. Develop social situations that will provide opportunity for an intermix of ages and family systems. The church can function as an extended family for the single who has never married, the widowed, or the child or teenager who must make it without a concerned parent or parents. Different generations no longer live together in most of

America, so any sense of community or intergenerational family needs to be provided by the church.

David and Vera Mace writing in *The Sacred Fire* cautioned that when the church becomes highly organized, segregating people by gender, age, marital status, and activity, central unity is lost. The church is no longer a family but an institution: "Certainly singles need a chance to get together; so do married couples, teenagers and retirees. But the great value of a family is that all its members, at various stages in the life cycle, may reach a loving and caring understanding of one another's joys and sorrows, hopes and fears."[1]

"The Great Family Gathering," a once-a-month Sunday evening dinner and program at Temple Baptist Church in Portland, Oregon, allows the mingling of all ages, even pre-schoolers. Sometimes attendees draw a number as they come in. This assigns them to their round table of eight. Thus cliques are broken up and people eat and talk with those they don't see very often. However, freedom of choice is important too. In city life, dinner may be the only extended social time with some friends from across the miles.

Four. If there is a seniors' group meeting regularly in the church, the pastoral or lay leadership can schedule periodic speaking and teaching times on subjects of specific concern to them. Many of the widowed will be present here. These can be abbreviated times during their regular social meetings, special meetings, or occasional seminars. In smaller churches and communities, offer ministry to a community senior group or host the meetings, thus broadening ministry opportunities.

Five. Develop other ministries to the widowed, such as financial planning, goal setting, premarital counseling, support groups, grief therapy seminars, Bible study groups, travel groups for both local and distant trips, and a telephone buddy system.

The telephone can be a great tool for checking daily just to be sure a person is well. One large church also uses the phone specifically for the newly widowed. The widowed are expected to select three individuals from a list of persons who are willing to talk to them at specific times each day. These volunteers have walked the lonely road to recovery after a loss. Part of the therapy program is to keep the newly widowed talking through the things they are struggling with.

Six. The role of minister to senior adults demands more than a retired minister (or a young active one) who wants to provide activities for retired people. A strong counseling background and the ability to challenge and direct seniors' physical, spiritual, and financial resources into satisfying service is essential. Most important for our purposes, a minister to senior adults must be able to provide a worthy ministry to the widowed.

Seven. Part of the specific teaching needed for the widowed of any age is the assurance that it is okay to remarry, as long as it is within biblical parameters. This is especially important for seniors because this was often considered socially inappropriate in their past. If they choose not to remarry or the opportunity is not theirs, then they may need help in developing as full a life as possible and avoiding social withdrawal.

Eight. Within the context of the church's educational and counseling program, adult children can be helped to understand the dynamics at work in middle and later decades. Children of any age can learn not to be threatened by remarriage, that it may be appropriate for a parent or grandparent. A remarriage of widowed persons in the church offers an opportunity to discuss the subject with various age groups.

Nine. Seminaries need to take the lead. Young pastors cannot be expected to have insight about the lives and needs of seniors, particularly the widowed. Even middle-aged pastors may not have the background needed. But the seminaries can begin to help; some are developing courses on the subject. According to *Christianity Today*, St. Paul United Methodist School of Theology in Kansas City, Missouri is the first seminary in the country to have a specific teaching position on gerontology and ministry to senior adults.[2]

As recently as 1990, the Association of Theological Seminaries (ATS) had no information on any other school with such an endowed chair. Information from the ATS and various seminaries indicates larger schools are taking steps to correct this situation. One school has twelve courses on the subject, five of which are built into the core curriculum.

A seminary professor commented that study in the field will need to be motivated by denominational leaders. Students must be encouraged to take courses in ministry to mature adults. His seminary offered some of these as electives, but the professor blamed our youth-oriented culture for the fact that no one enrolled in the classes.

One illustration of the huge demographic shift taking place in this country is that since 1985, there have been more people age sixty-five and over than those eighteen and younger. By 2025, Americans over sixty-five will outnumber teenagers by more than two to one.[3] Present and future pastors need to be prepared to minister to seniors, including the increasing number who will remarry after widowhood. Other seminaries will need to follow the example of the Kansas City school.

NEEDED: UNSELFISH COOPERATION

A complete ministry to the widowed, from bereavement through possible remarriage, can be offered only by the largest churches. But if the widowed and remarried will ask their church leaders to read this book and strongly encourage their congregations to act on suggestions in this chapter, some changes can begin to occur.

FOUR STEPS EVERY CONGREGATION CAN TAKE:

1. Develop whatever ministries to the widowed the church is capable of supporting.
2. If there is no existing program, develop a community cooperative program with other agencies in a small population center.
3. Work with other like-minded congregations to build a ministry to the widowed.
4. Put the welfare of the widowed above the fear of losing a member or two. If your church cannot develop a needed ministry, recommend that widowed persons become involved in another church's program, even if they must travel to another city. Such a spirit of love and compassion will never go unrewarded.

Appendix

The following three lists give helpful information about the similarities and differences between widowed and divorced people in various areas of life.

PATTERNS OF ADJUSTMENT FOR WIDOWED AND DIVORCED PERSONS

(Adapted from unpublished material by consulting psychologist Dr. Kenneth D. Barringer of Sheboygan, Wisconsin.)

DIVORCED PERSONS	WIDOWED PERSONS
1. Ego loss. Damaged self-concept.	1. No ego loss. Ego support.
2. Frantic rush for new companionship to restore ego loss.	2. Little desire for new companionship because of grief.
3. Some sexual experimentation to restore ego loss.	3. Awful sense of separation, but little sexual experimentation.
4. Rejection of former spouse.	4. Memory focus on loved one, usually pleasant.
5. Anger and resentment against actions of former spouse.	5. Bitterness over injustice of death or toward the loved one (he did not take care of himself).

DIVORCED PERSONS	WIDOWED PERSONS
6. Terrible loneliness. Learning to live alone if you did not receive custody of the children.	6. Loneliness dimmed by presence of children and much support from others.
7. Presence of partner in visitation forces review of difficult past.	7. Glorification of past and a treasuring of memories.
8. Pattern of use of children as pawns in angry disputes with former mate or as information sources (spies).	8. Children are seen now as more important and valued because they help continue the family structure.
9. Children's feelings are not always considered in the action because parents' emotions are overwhelming.	9. Need of children and their feelings are usually valued and often paramount because they offer security.
10. Children have deep reaction of guilt, rejection, and anger.	10. Children feel grief, loneliness, and resentment over exit of deceased person.
11. The continued battle between former partners can be constant and hard on the nerves.	11. No fencing between partners because there is only one left.
12. Divorced face constant pressure for financial support since the settlement often falls short of the real need.	12. Widow often does not have as critical a financial pressure because of financial assistance through Social Security.
13. Strong need for affection. Frequent rejection or avoidance of divorced by friends and family intensify this need.	13. Need for love and affection not as intense because of happy memories, much support from family and friends.

DIVORCED PERSONS	WIDOWED PERSONS
14. Divorced feel they have an edge over widowed in competition for new partner. Date more often.	14. Widowed view divorced as competitor for available partners. They date less often.
15. Confusion over who should be future spouse and where and how failure occurred in first marriage.	15. Recollection of happy events in marriage. Blotting out negative aspects in relationship.
16. Desire for early remarriage. Short engagements.	16. Desire to remarry not as intense. Far fewer widows remarry.

PAPERWORK AND ATTORNEYS

(Provided by the 1990 remarriage conference at New Hope Community Church, Portland, Oregon.)

DIVORCED PERSONS	WIDOWED PERSONS
1. Gathering of information needed to substantiate case for ownership of certain properties and other material possessions and for determining amount of spouse and child support.	1. There are mountains of paperwork to go through, fill out, mail, and file when your mate dies (insurances, Social Security, property titles, taxes, retirement).
2. Can be a great deal of manipulation and litigation.	2. Usually no hassles with family members over finances. (This changes many times at remarriage.)

DIVORCED PERSONS	WIDOWED PERSONS
3. Average divorce will cost in attorney's fees from $2,500 on up.	3. Most attorneys are willing to bill you by the hour for advice and legal help needed.
4. Both partners usually lose a great deal financially in divorce.	4. Many times there is financial gain if the deceased had insurance and a will.
5. Many women and their children end up living far below the standard they have been used to.	5. Widowed persons with children under age 18 will often get more monthly support per child from Social Security than those from divorce.
6. Most divorced women with dependent children must work in order to survive financially.	6. Many times the widow will be able to stay at home and be a full-time mom until children are older.

PHYSICAL PROBLEMS

(Provided by the 1990 remarriage conference at New Hope Community Church, Portland, Oregon.)

DIVORCED PERSONS	WIDOWED PERSONS
1. Sleeplessness.	1. May sleep a lot. Sign of depression.
2. Pains in the stomach.	2. All kinds of physical problems develop.
3. Urge to keep moving, doing something, running.	3. Overwhelming tiredness and inertia set in (especially if loved one has had a prolonged illness).
4. Waves of feeling rejected or anger result in rash behavior and decisions.	4. Feel unable to move and unable to make decisions. Tend to rely on others to make decisions for them.

Notes

INTRODUCTION

1. *Demographic Supplement of the* U.S. *Census Bureau, Marriage and Family Statistics Branch*, March 1989 ed.

2. U.S. Department of Health and Human Services, National Center for Health Statistics, *Monthly Vital Statistics Report* (April 3, 1990): 13.

3. Ibid., 15.

CHAPTER 1: COMING ALIVE AGAIN

1. Sheldon Vanauken, A *Severe Mercy* (San Francisco: Harper & Row, 1977), 180.

2. Granger E. Westberg, *Good Grief* (Philadelphia: Fortress, 1973).

3. C. S. Lewis, A *Grief Observed* (New York: Bantam, 1976), 72.

4. Ibid., 61.

5. Elisabeth Elliot, *Loneliness* (Nashville: Oliver Nelson, 1988), 146.

CHAPTER 2: THE DATING GAME

1. Jane Burgess Kohn and Willard K. Kohn, *The Widower* (Boston: Beacon, 1978), 87.

2. Ibid., 88.

3. Jim A. Talley and Bobbie Reed, *Too Close, Too Soon* (Nashville: Nelson, 1982), 35–41.

4. Jann Mitchell, "Take a Time Out and Try Some Non-Dating," *The Oregonian* (November 27, 1988).

CHAPTER 3: ME? SEE A COUNSELOR?

1. To explore the possibility of regional differences in experiences or attitudes among the widowed, a limited survey, not a scientific study, was conducted using a six-page questionnaire. It was distributed to a few senior, remarried widowed persons in each of eleven large churches across the country. No regional differences were noted.

2. "The Second Time Around: Realities of Remarriage," U.S. *News and World Report* (January 29, 1990): 50.

3. Mel Krantzler, *Learning to Love Again* (New York: Thomas Y. Crowell, 1977), 195.

CHAPTER 4: COURTING AND DECIDING

1. "How America Has Run Out of Time," *Time* (April 24, 1989): 59.

2. 1 Corinthians 6:13–20; 7; Ephesians 5:3–7; and Song of Solomon are among many Scripture passages to review.

CHAPTER 5: PROTECTING YOUR ASSETS

1. *Your Legal Guide to Marriage and Other Relationships* (Chicago: American Bar Association, Public Education Division, 1989).

2. "From Wedlock to Deadlock? How to Negotiate a Prenup," *Money* (April 1990): 21.

3. "Retirement," *Money* (September 1989): 146.

4. Contact the American Association of Retired Persons, Publications Department, 1909 K Street N.W., Washington, D.C. 20049, and ask for *Decision Making, Incapacity and the Elderly*, published in 1987. Or see the article by Jan Rosen on page 18 of the July 22, 1989 *New York Times*.

CHAPTER 6: MONEY, MONEY, MONEY

1. Social Security Administration Publication #13-11727.

2. George C. Myers and Barbara Foley Wilson, *Marriage Trends and Patterns of Older Americans* (Washington, D.C.: Duke University and the National Center for Health Statistics, n.d.). Paper addresses trends from 1970–83.

3. Social Security Administration Publication #05-10077, January 1988.

CHAPTER 7: IN SICKNESS AND IN HEALTH

1. "Growing Old: Long Term Care," *Pacific Northwest Magazine,* (March 1987): 67.

2. "Data Aids Image of Nursing Homes," *The Oregonian* (January 11, 1978): A6.

3. Ruth Harriet Jacobs and Barbara H. Vinick, *Re-Engagement in Later Life* (Stamford, Conn.: Greylock, 1979), 225.

4. Jane Burgess Kohn and Willard K. Kohn, *The Widower* (Boston: Beacon, 1978), 154.

5. Charles P. Sabatino, *Health Care Powers of Attorney* (Washington, D.C.: American Bar Association and AARP, 1990).

CHAPTER 8: SPEAKING OF SEX . . .

1. Bernard D. Starr and Marcella Baker Weiner, *Sex and Sexuality in the Mature Years* (New York: Stein and Day, 1981), 6.

2. Ibid., 179.

3. Jim Talley and Bobbie Reed, *Too Close, Too Soon* (Nashville: Nelson, 1982), 44.

4. John White, *Eros Defiled* (Downers Grove, Ill.: InterVarsity Press, 1977), 21.

5. Ruth B. Weg, ed., *Sex in the Later Years* (New York: Academic Press, 1983), 14.

6. Robert N. Butler and Myrna I. Lewis, *Love and Sex After Sixty* (New York: Harper and Row, 1977), 4.

7. Richard Morris and Loretta Morris, "Aging in an Adolescent Culture," *Theology News and Notes* (June 1981): 20.

8. Butler, *Love and Sex After Sixty,* 95.

9. Ruth Harriett Jacobs and Barbara H. Vinick, *Re-engagement in Later Life: Re-employment and Remarriage* (Stamford, Conn.: Greylock, 1979), 234.

10. Butler, *Love and Sex After Sixty*, 126.

11. William F. Harley, *His Needs, Her Needs* (Old Tappan, N.J.: Revell, 1986), 50.

CHAPTER 9: WHAT WILL THE CHILDREN SAY?

1. Jane Burgess Kohn and Willard K. Kohn, *The Widower* (Boston: Beacon, 1978), 98.

CHAPTER 10: WHAT ABOUT YOUNG CHILDREN?

1. "Step by Step," *Newsweek: The 21st Century Family* (Special Edition: Winter/Spring 1990): 27.

2. "Ministry to Stepfamilies," *Theology, News and Notes* (June 1988): 17.

3. Ibid.

4. Andre Bustanoby, *The Ready-Made Family* (Grand Rapids: Zondervan, 1982), 113.

5. "The Second Time Around: Realities of Remarriage," U.S. *News & World Report* (January 29, 1990): 50.

CHAPTER 12: WHEN IT'S TIME TO SAY "I DO"

1. George W. Knight, *The Second Marriage Guidebook* (Brentwood, Tenn.: JM Publications, 1984).

2. Amy Vanderbilt, *The Amy Vanderbilt Complete Book of Etiquette: Revised and Expanded by Letitia Baldridge* (Garden City: Doubleday, 1978), 255. This reference is in chapter 21, "Second and Subsequent Marriages," and is well worth exploring again or for the first time. Further information will be found in chapter 63, "Gift Ideas for all Occasions."

CHAPTER 13: ROOF OFF, WALLS DOWN

1. Mel Krantzler, *Learning to Love Again* (New York: Thomas Y. Crowell, 1977), 190.
2. H. Norman Wright, *Before You Marry* (Eugene, Ore.: Harvest House, 1988), 61.
3. Elaine Simpson Mynatt, *Remarriage Reality* (Knoxville, Tenn.: Elm Publications, 1984), 40–41.

CHAPTER 15: THE CHURCH AND THE WIDOWED

1. David Mace and Vera Mace, *The Sacred Fire: Christian Marriage Through the Ages* (Nashville: Abingdon, 1986), 269.
2. "The Graying of America," *Christianity Today* (November 6, 1987): 17.
3. Ken Dychtwald, *Age Wave* (New York: Bantam, 1990), 21.

Bibliography

Burkett, Larry. *Answers to Your Family's Financial Questions.* Pomona, Calif.: Focus On The Family, 1987. Practical help from one who writes and lectures widely in this field.

Bustanoby, Andre. *The Ready-Made Family.* Grand Rapids: Zondervan, 1982. Practical counsel on incest and the stepfamily. Chapter 9, "What to Expect From a Stepchild," is especially valuable.

Butler, Robert N., and Myrna I. Lewis. *Love and Sex After Sixty: A Guide for Men and Women for Their Later Years.* New York: Harper and Row, 1977. A helpful book, although some philosophy and practices will not be acceptable to most evangelicals.

Dychtwald, Ken, and Joe Flower. *Age Wave.* New York: Bantam, 1990. Entire book excellent for statistics and trend projections on aging of U.S. population and its effects on all of us.

Elliot, Elisabeth. *Loneliness.* Nashville: Oliver Nelson, 1988. Highly recommended for those grieving over loss by death or divorce and all who suffer loneliness from any cause.

Graham, Billy. *Facing Death and the Life After*. Waco, Tex.: Word, 1987. Simple, straight to the heart with ample illustrations throughout the book. Note chapter 8, "Groping Through Grief."

Harley, William F. *His Needs/Her Needs*. Old Tappan, N.J.: Revell, 1986. Excellent on relational skills within marriage.

Hocking, David. *Marrying Again: A Guide for Christians*. Old Tappan, N.J.: Revell, 1983. Biblical treatment on the issues confronting younger remarrieds and those thinking of remarrying.

Howard, Grant. *The Trauma of Transparency*. Portland, Ore.: Multnomah Press, 1979. Urges transparency in communication of all kinds. Good study book for groups.

Jacobs, Ruth Harriet, and Barbara H. Vinick. *Re-Engagement in Later Life*. Stamford, Conn.: Greylock Publishers, 1979.

Johnson, Laurene. *Divorced Kids*. Nashville: Nelson, 1990. Practical help for the blended family.

Juroe, David J., and Bonnie B. Juroe. *Successful Stepparenting*. Old Tappan, N.J.: Revell, 1983. The authors write from a biblical perspective, using personal experience as well as insight gained as professional counselors.

Knight, George W. *The Second Marriage Guidebook*. Brentwood, Tenn.: JM Publications, 1984. Practical answers on wedding etiquette and other aspects of the second marriage.

Kohn, Jane Burgess, and Willard K. Kohn. *The Widower*. Boston: Beacon Press, 1978. The chronicle of a man experiencing loss, grief, adjustment to life, and remarriage.

Krantzler, Mel. *Learning to Love Again*. New York: Thomas Y. Crowell Co., 1977.

Lewis, C. S. A *Grief Observed*. New York: Harper and Row, 1977. Faith renewed in the face of grief as related by this premier author.

Mace, David, and Vera Mace. *The Sacred Fire: Christian Marriage Through the Ages*. Nashville: Abingdon, 1986. A great historical overview. An academic, well-documented work.

MacGregor, Malcolm, and Stanley G. Baldwin. *Your Money Matters*. Minneapolis: Bethany House, 1988.

Martin, Judith. *Miss Manners' Guide to Excruciatingly Correct Behavior*. New York: Atheneum, 1982. Chapter on weddings pp. 317-395.

Mason, Florence. *To Love Again: Intimate Relationships After Sixty*. San Francisco: Gateway Books, 1989. Easy, humorous reading with cartoons, focusing on the older widowed and their sexual needs. Based on interviews.

Mynatt, Elaine Simpson. *Remarriage Reality*. Knoxville, Tenn.: Elm Publications, 1984.

Richards, Larry. *Remarriage, A Healing Gift from God*. Waco, Tex.: Word, 1981. An open attitude on remarriage by an evangelical. For those struggling with the biblical perspective.

Starr, Bernard D., and Marcella Baker Weiner. *Sex and Sexuality in the Mature Years*. New York: Stein and Day, 1981. An investigative research work with some data worth noting.

Talley, Jim, and Bobbie Reed. *Too Close, Too Soon*. Nashville: Nelson, 1982. Excellent on dating, courting, and how long to wait. Directed to younger audience, but worth reviewing.

Vanauken, Sheldon. A *Severe Mercy*. New York: Harper and Row, 1977. Awarded the Gold Medallion Book Award, this beautifully written, personal love story tenderly touches the cords of tragedy and grief.

Vanderbilt, Amy. *The Amy Vanderbilt Complete Book of Etiquette: Revised and Expanded by Letitia Baldridge*. Garden City: Doubleday, 1978. Chapter 21 on second marriages.

Walker, Glynnis. *Second Wife, Second Best?* Toronto: Doubleday, Canada. Good insights on how the second wife may sometimes be treated or how she sees herself.

Weg, Ruth B., Ed., *Sexuality in the Later Years*. New York: Academic Press, 1983.

Westberg, Granger E. *Good Grief*. Philadelphia: Fortress, 1973. This volume continues to be a basic reference on the subject and is especially noted for its ten steps.

Wheat, Ed, and Gaye Wheat. *Intended for Pleasure*. Old Tappan, N.J.: Revell, 1981. Christian perspective. One chapter, "Sex After 60, . . . 70, . . . 80," is directed to the senior.

White, John. *Eros Defiled*. Downers Grove, Ill.: InterVarsity Press, 1977. This associate professor of psychiatry offers helpful analysis of variant sexual practices.

Wright, H. Norman. *Before You Remarry*. Eugene, Ore.: Harvest House, 1988. Learning to communicate before marriage and understanding issues. As with almost all books on remarriage, the audience is the divorced, but it's valuable for all, especially younger dating couples. A self-help workbook.

————. *How to Speak Your Spouse's Language*. Old Tappan, N.J.: Revell, 1986. How to communicate within marriage.

Young, Amy Ross. *By Death or Divorce: It Hurts to Lose*. Denver: Accent, 1976. Excellent comparison of the two losses.